The Search for Truth

The Search for Truth

The Life and Teaching Methods of the Indian Sufi Shaykh Hazrat Maulvi Muhammad Sa'id Khan (r)

by

Shaykh al-Tariqat Hazrat Azad Rasool (r)

FONS VITAE

First published in 2010 by
Fons Vitae
49 Mockingbird Valley Drive
Louisville, KY 40207
http://www.fonsvitae.com

Library of Congress Control Number: 2009933710

ISBN 9781891785436

Printed in Canada

This book was typeset by Neville Blakemore, Jr.

DEDICATION

To all sincere students who are in search of Truth

Contents

Foreword

O reader! It is only appropriate to begin with the largest possible context, in the name of God, the most compassionate and merciful. In Reality, that Largest Context called God is beyond words, gender, or attributes. Since we too often live in the cramped boxes of smaller worldly contexts, that is the only way we can conceive of that Greatest Beyond. Thus, books and scriptures are written accordingly.

But the realm of conceiving and of language is that of a very small box – the dualistic mind. The book you have in your hands right now is about going beyond the illusory dualistic worldly reality (while living in it), hence the expression "to be in the world but not of it." It is about realizing and awakening to this Largest Context. It is an invitation to experience ultimate Reality as it is – One. This book is about those who have aspired to and have experienced God's Oneness, diligently cultivating a unitary consciousness. The Search for Truth goes on to explain the verified methods available to experience God that have been followed by Naqshbandi-Mujaddidi Sufis. In between the written lines the reader is called to our common human birthright – the human experience of consciously experiencing the vastness of the Largest Context, the goal of all spiritual quests (although the vocabulary differs across religio-spiritual traditions). In Sufi terms, the Path is about becoming close to God.

Historically, "Sufi" was first used in an eighth-century Islamic context for ascetics wearing woolen cloaks – like their Christian counterparts – in the deserts of the Near East. Eventually by the tenth century this activity developed into a branch of the Islamic religious sciences – what has become known as Sufism in the West. In the Sunni world (the mainstream Muslim community) "the process of becoming a Sufi" (*tasawwuf*), and in the Iranian Shi'i world "theoretical mysticism" (*'irfan*), are conflated in the English term "Sufism." The activities of Sufis are generally acknowledged by historians to be responsible for the spread of Islam in the Eastern Islamic world, including present-day Turkey, India, Indonesia, and Africa. Investigation into the historical processes of Islamization, still going on today, indicate that the Sufi message is more expansive than, yet inclusive of, the doctrinal, orthopraxic religion known as Islam. That is, although Sufism historically has been practiced almost exclusively by Muslims, it has also gone beyond the human-created boundaries of the religion of Islam to include anyone who seeks to submit to God, the technical meaning of *muslim* in Arabic. In *The Search for Truth* the Sufism described is explicitly one that is rooted in Islamic ritual practices, hence the term 'Islamic Sufism'.

How is Sufism central to the practice of Islam? The easiest way to answer this is to quote the famous hadith of the Prophet (S) known as Gabriel's Hadith (hadith are the recorded sayings and actions of the Prophet Muhammad (S)). It is so famous that it is the first hadith in some hadith collections. In shortened form it tells about a man with very white clothing and very black hair coming up to the Prophet (S) and his companions. No mark of travel was visible on him, and no one recognized him. Sitting down before the Prophet (S) he said, "Tell me, Muhammad, about submission to God (*islam*)." He replied, "Submission means that you should bear witness that there is no god but God and that Muhammad is God's messenger, that you should perform the ritual prayer, pay alms, fast during Ramadan, and make the pilgrimage to the House if you are able to go there." The man said, "You have spoken the truth." Then he said, "Now tell me about faith (*iman*)." Muhammad replied, "Faith means that you have faith in God, his angels, his books, his messengers, and the last day and that you have faith in the measuring out, both its good and its evil." Remarking that the Prophet had spoken the truth, he then said, "Now tell me about doing what is beautiful (*ihsan*)." Muhammad replied, "Doing what is beautiful means that you should worship God as if you see him, for even if you do not see him, he sees you." When the man left, Muhammad (S) informed his astonished companions that the angel Gabriel had come to teach them about their religion.

Here was religion in a nutshell: what one does (*islam*), what one thinks (*iman*), and what one intends in one's heart (*ihsan*). The point here is that each of these three religious dimensions is interconnected with each other dimension like a tree's roots, branches, and fruit. Being a perfected or complete human being involves an integration of these three dimensions. Sufism is that third dimension, the fruit of action and faith. Those Muslims who deny Sufism do not recognize this integral "heart dimension" in Islam. Such a three-dimensional conception of Islam assumes that different persons have varying potential and ability for spiritual accomplishment. The vast majority of Muslims seek salvation through their daily practices, informed by a faith commitment. Sufism, on the other hand, encompasses the activities working toward the field of consciousness and experience represented by acting in a beautiful manner. Such an enterprise assumes a firm foundation in faith and in the practice of submitting to God before achieving an extraordinary degree of proximity to God. Surely not all who call themselves Sufis are able to achieve this advanced goal and not all of the few who reach this stage are necessarily Sufis.

Another oft-mentioned triad associated with explicating Sufism is Islamic law (*shari'a*), the Sufi path (*tariqa*), and reality (*haqiqa*). For Muslims, Islamic law represents the wide path outlining (what are perceived to be) the timeless God-given rules that govern everyday life for all humans. It is the path leading to salvation. The Sufi path is a narrower path leading to reality, the experience of the Ultimate. These three interrelated aspects of Islam have been depicted as the one circle of Islamic law with a multiplicity of radii or Sufi paths leading to the reality at the center. In transformative terms, Islamic law is medical science, the Sufi path is preventing disease and taking medicine, and experiencing reality is eternally perfect health. The latter metaphor implies a necessary doctor or guide who has eternally perfect health. These triads clearly show the role of Islamic ritual practices in Islamic Sufism.

The practice of Sufism involves the inner aspect of Islam (the submission to God/Ultimate reality), including spiritual transformation and character development. To the extent that Sufis desire closeness or intimacy with God, Sufism can be roughly translated as Islamic mysticism. Insofar as these interior experiences and transformations are not apparent to others (in contrast to woolen clothing) Sufism can be said to be the esoteric aspect of Islam. From the mystical perspective, Sufism is the study and cultivation of one's actual experience with God. In a more poetic fashion, one could say that Sufism is the intentional act of plunging into a wave from the Infinite Ocean and being drawn back with it toward the Eternal Source.

A Sufi's experience-based religious authority has often been contested by jurists focusing on Islamic law whose knowledge is based upon book learning (though one can be both a Sufi and a jurist). Jurists are interested in the external symbols and outward behavior that are associated with maintaining and outwardly legitimizing Islamic social structures through a system of law, schools, and mosques. The jurist's expression of religion integrates and stabilizes society. Islamic law is the "husk" that protects, legitimizes, and tempers the precious "kernel" of contemplative practice.

This spiritual practice is required for the integration and stabilization of the outer social structure and presumes movement, change, and transformation within the individual. Instead of jihad as war, Sufis stress the "inner struggling (*jihad*) in the path of God," controlling the desires and ignorance of one's ego, the sense of I-ness (*nafs*). The transformation process implies an unfolding, a transcending of prior states and perceptions. Often this transformation in the Sufi environment is associated with the spiritual experiences connected with performance of Sufi contemplative practices.

In a traditional pre-modern Sufi setting involving an authentic teaching context, a level of moral and ethical development and integration into society was required of the aspirant before the spiritual guide taught him or her contemplative practices. If this basic development was not in place then basic (and often uncomfortable) foundational work was given first. This was not only because of the teacher's time constraints but also because few people really wanted to confront their egos. It is much easier to participate in a 'feel good' escape from everyday life under the guise of 'spiritual development'. The practices outlined in this book involve the student dealing with the 'hard ego stuff' of his or her life under the close supervision of a qualified teacher. Therefore the first step on the path of Sufism is to find a qualified and harmonious teacher. At some point one formally makes a commitment through an initiation ritual (or looks for another teacher), and then proceeds to incorporate a contemplative discipline into one's life.

Initiation in Sufism is modeled after the Companions pledging allegiance to Muhammad (S) at Hudaybiya in 628. The Qur'anic verse associated with this reads, 'Those who swear allegiance to you [Muhammad] actually swear allegiance to God. God's hand is over their hands.' (48:10). Sufi lineages are important in Sufism because they establish the unbroken tradition of the handshake of initiation going back to Muhammad (S). Spiritual lineages, continuous chains of pious Sufis leading back to the Prophet (S), were also a way for Sufis to meet juristic challenges to their authority. By the eleventh century a number of international pan-Islamic Sufi lineages named after their founder figures came into existence, including the Kazaruniyya or Murshidiyya from Abu Ishaq al-Kazaruni (d. 1035 in Shiraz) and the Qadiriyya lineage from 'Abdulqadir al-Jilani (d. 1166 in Baghdad), the most widely spread lineage in the Islamic world. Other major lineages include the Suhrawardi lineage from Abu Hafs Suhrawardi (d. 1234 in Baghdad); the Chishti lineage in India from Mu'inuddin Chishti (d. 1236 Ajmer, Rajasthan, India); the Naqshbandi lineage from Baha'uddin Naqshband (d. 1389 Bukhara, Uzbekistan); the Mevlevi lineage from Jalaluddin Rumi (d. 1273 in Konya, Turkey), named after the Turkish form of the honorific, *maulana*, the name by which Turks refer to him; and the Naqshbandiyya-Mujaddidiyya lineage from Ahmad Sirhindi (d. 1634 Sirhind, India), the practices of which are addressed in this book.

These lineages prospered through the institutionalization of subsidized Sufi lodges throughout the Islamic world where Sufis endeavoured to replicate the model community of the Prophet (S) and his companions. A set of rituals and practices governed life in this new institution – justified on the basis of the prophetic sunna (what the Prophet is said to have done). The author of *The Search for Truth*, the late Hazrat Azad Rasool (may his inner heart be sanctified), who passed from this earth in 2006, was the thirty-third link in the initiatic chain going back to the Prophet (S) via Abu Bakr as-Siddiq (d. 634), Baha'uddin Naqshband, Ahmad Sirhindi, and Adam Banuri (d. 1644 Medina), Ahmad Sirhindi's most spiritually advanced successor.

What is noteworthy about Hazrat's lineage is how his great grandfather pir (his shaykh's grand shaykh) Shaykh Sayyid 'Abdul Bari Shah (d. 1900 Bandel, India) began to restructure the Mujaddidi practices and initiation procedure for modern times. Hazrat goes into detail how his own shaykh, Maulvi Muhammad Sai'd Khan, imparted the teachings and practices of the orders in ways that were responsive to the changing needs and capacities of the seekers. Hazrat gives the reader a sense of what it means to proceed on the Sufi path. The contemplative practices as described in the book take into account the modern difficulties that both Muslim and non-Muslim aspirants to the Sufi path may encounter. There is no longer any "East" or "West" in Hazrat's lineage. Hazrat's students and their Sufi communities are on every continent.

In early February 2000, a friend and I took a long rickshaw ride from one side of New Delhi to Jamia Nagar so we could meet Hazrat Azad Rasool. Although it could not have been more than an hour or two, it was a meeting that has left a lasting impression on me beyond his gracious and gentle demeanor. The mosque at The Institute of Search for Truth still had not been completed. What has become a small complex of buildings near the mosque symbolizes the global spread of teachings done by a soft-spoken, modest gentleman whose mission has been to awaken human hearts. Hazrat, in the early stages of his diligent search for Truth, probably had no idea of the role he was going to play in facilitating God's work. Likewise you, the reader, have no idea of how a small book like this can change your life. The worst that can happen is that nothing will happen. The rule of the conditioned ego will simply continue, hour after hour, day after day, year after year. The other alternative is that something else will happen. It is your choice. I invite you to find out.

Arthur F. Buehler
Senior Lecturer
Victoria University
Wellington, New Zealand

Editors' Preface

In Sufism, biographies describing the lives of the saints support the practical learning a seeker or student must undertake with the guidance of a Sufi shaykh. This biography of Hazrat Maulvi Muhammad Sai'd Khan (r) is the second book published in English by Hazrat Azad Rasool (r).[1,2] In this new book, the author supplements a selection of Hazrat Maulvi Muhammad Sai'd Khan's (r) writings, letters and discourses with his own writing to contextualize and provide insight into the life and teaching methods of his shaykh. This original material, translated here into English from the Urdu,[3] has been selected from a larger body of material that was transcribed and collected by the author over the course of thirty years, whilst travelling and working with his teacher across the Indian Subcontinent.

The original material and transcribed dialogues between Hazrat Maulvi Muhammad Sai'd Khan (r) and his students belong to a body of Sufi teaching that often remains oral and exists only within the practice of Sufism itself. The rarity of such important teaching material cannot be overestimated. These texts contain deeply practical information and invaluable insights into Sufism, Islam, and the practices of the Naqshbandi-Mujaddidi order, usually inaccessible to the uninitiated seeker. The narrative structure weaves transcriptions, personal testimony, and biographical accounts into what it is hoped readers will experience as a cohesive and generous unfolding of what it is, and might be, to undertake the challenge of growing closer to God.

The biography is presented here as a tribute to a great saint and teacher and as a contemporary essay on the practice and teaching of Sufism as practiced by the shaykhs of the Naqshbandi-Mujaddidi order, of which the author Hazrat Azad Rasool (r), was a master and teacher. It also provides a rare insight into the relationship of a Sufi shaykh to his students (*murid*s) and makes clear to the reader the vital role of the teacher in relation to a student's spiritual progress. The detailed explanation of his shaykh's teaching methodology is

1. The abbreviation (r) (Ar. *rahmat Allah 'alayhi/'alayha*) is a pious blessing meaning, 'May God have mercy on him/her' and is used after the names of spiritually elevated individuals who have passed away.

2. The first book is *Turning Toward the Heart: Awakening to the Sufi Way* by Shaykh al-Tariqat Hazrat Azad Rasool (Louisvsille, KY: Fons Vitae, 2002).

3. Azad Rasool, *Sawanih-i hayat-i Hadarat Maulwi Muhammad Sa'id Khan Sahib (r)* (New Delhi: Idara-yi Talash-i Haqq, 2003).

intended to give the uninitiated seeker an accurate sense of the work of the Naqshbandi-Mujaddidi order of Sufism. In writing this new biography, he himself extends this tradition of innovation in teaching.

Carefully written specifically to address those Westerners seeking a genuine spiritual path and a teacher, this book intends to inspire the student and seeker alike through the recounting of two inextricably linked lives lived in and with God. It is a book about the teaching and learning process itself, the process of spiritual refinement and what it means to be successful on the Naqshbandi-Mujaddidi Sufi path. Read on its own, this book is an important source for those seeking to understand something of the work of the Sufi path, but, as the author explains in the text, it can in no way replace the guidance and attention of the shaykh. Words are only the means by which an individual can attain spiritual affinity; true spiritual affinity (*nisbat*) can only be achieved through those shaykhs that have the authority to teach.

*

Hazrat Azad Rasool (r) passed away on the 7th of November 2006. He spent more than fifty-five years of his life working tirelessly to spread the message of Sufism across the world, particularly the West. Hazrat travelled not only through the length and breadth of India but also to Australia, East Asia, Europe and America, and today his following includes seekers from all over the world. The number of seekers who have benefited from Hazrat's (r) teaching continues to grow and his work continues through the Institute of Search for Truth and the School of Sufi Teaching (www.sufischool.org), which have branches in several countries. As is the tradition in Sufi orders, the work continues uninterrupted. Hazrat's son and deputy (*khalifa*), Shaykh Hamid Hasan now leads the Institute of Search for Truth and the School of Sufi Teaching and provides initiation and guidance to people on the path of Sufism.

The last three years of Hazrat's (r) life were devoted to working on this book, which contains an account of his own quest for Truth, his teacher's life, and the teachings of the order. Fluent in both English and Urdu, the author's attention to every last detail and decision taken in both the editing and translation processes involved in producing this biography has ensured the authenticity of the work. It was his dearest wish to reach out to seekers who were yearning for the Truth and he would keep reiterating the importance of this text to that effort. The editing and translation of the original Urdu material also reflects the work of many friends whose expertise and generosity have helped to shape the quality of this work. May Allah reward them for this. We are certain that this book will, as Hazrat intended, prove to be a source of guidance and blessings for seekers of Truth everywhere in the world.

Shazreh Hussain
Sukaina Mazhar
Tanya Usman
20 October 2008
London

Author's Preface

When I returned after completing my teaching degree in education from Allahabad, I was appointed lecturer at Jamia Training College, and it was there that I met Mr. Rauz ur-Rahman. When he heard of my anguished quest for Truth he advised me to meet with and seek guidance from Hazrat Maulvi Muhammad Sa'id Khan Sahib (r),[1] who was a teacher of Arabic at the Shibli School in Azamgarh and also a Sufi shaykh. Mr. Rauz ur-Rahman had great faith that with his advice and guidance I could find a solution, and as a drowning man clutches at straw, I immediately wrote a detailed letter to Hazrat. At the end of the letter I wrote that I had made every effort to understand the mystery of existence, to know Reality, and to find peace of mind. However, the more I had tried the more my anguish grew.

I wrote: "I have been longing to meet you ever since I heard about you. I hope what Mr. Rauz ur-Rahman has said is true and after meeting with you, I will not have to wander anymore in search of a guide and through your compassion and guidance I will understand Reality. That is my dearest hope and desire. I beseech you to

Make me inebriated like you,
Let me lose myself in you,
Cast a lightning glance on the self I have hoarded
And let me re-enact the story of Moses on Mount Sinai.
You are the cupbearer, the tavern, and the wine,
I am longing to be intoxicated; intoxicate me!
Inhabit my heart and soul
Or turn them into deserts
Rescue me from the prison of phenomena.
Make of me whatever you will
I dwell at your feet
There is nothing more I have to say.
Make of me whatever you please."

It so happened that after a few days, Hazrat (r) came to Mathura, Uttar Pradesh, in connection with a refresher course for teachers of eastern languages. I saw this as a great opportunity, and arrived in Mathura with Mr. Rauz ur-Rahman's letter of introduction. After learning that Hazrat was staying at a mosque, I entered the mosque

1. 'Hazrat' (Ar. *hadrat*) is an honorific used for spiritual teachers and leaders or shaykhs.

and saw from a distance a maulvi wearing a *lungi* (a cloth wrapped around the waist) and a round white cap, lying on the floor of a room with his hands under his head.[2] He rose when he saw me coming. I had thought that I would tell him about my state in great detail, but when I entered his presence I went into a trance and all I could say was, "Hazrat, I have been searching since I was a child; I have read whatever I could read; and I have done whatever I could do. I have looked everywhere but my goal has evaded me. Mr. Rauz ur-Rahman says you have such tremendous spiritual power that if you were to glance at clay, it would come to life. It is this hope that has brought me to your door. Please bestow your favor upon me." Hazrat listened to me quietly. After he had been quiet for some time he said, "This is a matter of experience. Begin and see what happens." Our meeting was brief but my heart was in a state of tumult. I was so deeply impressed with Hazrat that I spent the night in Mathura and started my training with him the next day.

It is my great good fortune that for nearly thirty years I had the honor of being with Hazrat whenever he was traveling and whenever he took up residence somewhere. If someone asked Hazrat a question in an assembly he usually answered in great detail and with divine inspiration. It was not possible to write down what Hazrat was saying in his holy presence though I did try a couple of times. Seeing that it distracted him, I gave up the practice. Subsequently, once the gathering had dispersed, I wrote down as soon as possible what Hazrat had said from memory. Hazrat knew this and sometimes when he had spoken on an important issue, he asked, "What have you written? Let me hear it." If I had made any mistakes, he corrected them. If I was not sure about something, I asked Hazrat before I wrote anything down and added whatever had been left out.

It was my great desire to publish Hazrat's biography with all his discourses and sayings while he was alive. This was not possible due to the many responsibilities and commitments that kept me occupied, and is a source of the deepest regret. Today, several years after Hazrat's demise, I have been able to present Hazrat's life and his method of imparting spiritual training to seekers in the shape of a biography. I have done my best to capture Hazrat's discourses, thoughts, and reflections in writing. To do justice to Hazrat's tower-

---

2. *Maulvi* is a title used to address someone who has been trained in the external religious sciences to some extent, and is commonly used in India when addressing the prayer leader.

ing and all-embracing personality in writing was a very difficult task for an unworthy person like me. If there is some error or oversight in my recounting of Hazrat's sayings, the reader must attribute it to my own limitations.

Everyone
who comes into this world
brings a reason for living with them.
Those who strive not
with deeds towards it,
are among the living dead.

Drench this universe
with the rain of your actions.
Only those who sow the seeds
of action
reap the fruit of bliss.

The destination is reached only
after suffering the hardships
of the journey.
Those who know the reality
of suffering are the ones
who will know joy.

Each suffering
carries a message of joy,
just like winter
holds out the promise of spring. He who flows on
like a river
is oblivious to the plains and mountains.

There is a treasure
that is distributed with abandon, in
the late hours of each night.
He who is awake, receives it
and he who sleeps,
loses it.

(*anon*)

Introduction: A Search for Truth

Even as a child I was given to introspection. I often thought about who we were, where we had come from, and the purpose of our existence. I wondered whether there was life after death. The question that occupied me most was whether creation was a well-thought-out design, the gift of a Creator, or simply the result of an arbitrary incident. I have spent most of my life contemplating and unraveling these questions.

I was born in Kankroli, a town near Udaipur, Rajasthan. In Kankroli there was a big Dawarkaji temple, a sacred place of pilgrimage for Hindus where *sadhus* and *sants* (Hindu ascetics and sages) often came. I was very impressed with the way they had renounced worldly comforts in the pursuit of Truth and wandered from place to place carrying their homes on their backs. I spent hours in conversation with the *sadhus* attempting to find answers to my questions.

My older brother, whom we used to call Dada Bhai, was actively involved in politics. Once, when one of the Congress leaders came to Udaipur, Dada Bhai took my elder brother Ismail and I to meet him. When he asked me my name, I told him it was Ghulam Rasool. In those days the freedom movement was at its height. On hearing my name, he said, "Don't say Ghulam Rasool, say Azad Rasool!"[1] Although I did not approve, my friends started to call me by this new name and soon this came to be the name I was known by.

In 1933 with the advice of this Congress leader and his recommendation for scholarships, Dada Bhai sent my brother Ismail and I to Jamia Millia Islamia, the national Muslim university in Delhi, for our education. I was very fortunate to get this opportunity because my own circumstances did not permit it. My education at Jamia began with my admission in Class Five. As I was used to Hindi and the medium of instruction at the Jamia was Urdu, I faced some difficulties in the beginning but later was able to catch up. My writing also improved under the guidance of Rustam-i Qalam (Master of the Pen) Ustad 'Ali Muhammad Khan, who taught calligraphy at the school.

In 1942 I completed my Bachelor of Arts degree. Since all subjects other than science were a compulsory part of the curriculum, I gained some understanding of the most important subjects. As a result, I felt no hesitation or difficulty in talking or writing about

1. '*Ghulam*' means servant; '*Azad*' means free.

whatever subject was under discussion. Jamia did not offer a Master of Arts, and its degree was not officially recognized, so I could not continue my education there. I managed instead to get the opportunity to do my MA in Philosophy at the Aligarh Muslim University and a Diploma of Teaching from Allahabad. I also undertook research on the religious thought of Hazrat Shaykh Ahmad Faruqi Sirhindi (r) (d. 1624), but due to certain circumstances could not complete it.

My student days were splendid. The discipline of the hostel, a frugal diet, the company and blessings of capable and dedicated teachers (Dr. Zakir Hussain, Dr. Sayyid 'Abid Hussain, Professor Muhammad Mujib, Professor E. J. Kallatt, Professor Muhammad Sarwar, Maulana Aslam Jairajpuri and others), and an equal focus on sports and studies all contributed to this.[2,3] I was appointed president of *Anjuman-i Ittihad*, the Students' Literary Association, and was also captain of the college hockey team for several years, having played hockey since my days at school. Due to my success in sports, and my scholarly achievements in education and literature, I was fortunate to enjoy the love and respect of the students and teachers alike.

As a student, I had already decided that as soon as I had completed my education, I would enter the world of journalism. I was deeply impressed by Maulana Azad's newspaper *Al-Hilal*, Maulana Muhammad 'Ali's *Comrade,* and Zafar 'Ali Khan's *Zamindar*. As soon as I had completed my BA from Jamia, I left for Lahore to pursue my dream. My teacher, Professor Muhammad Sarwar, was working in the field of journalism there. Professor Sarwar was the editor of *Ihsan*, a daily newspaper, and I was given the opportunity of working with him. Thanks to the professor, I also worked with Mr. Shafi'i, who was the joint editor of the English paper *Civil and Military Gazette.* Dr. Zakir Hussain had also written me a recommendation for Rana Jang Bahadur, an 'old boy' from Jamia who was the editor of the *Tribune*. As a result I also had the chance to work with him and gained a lot of experience.

---

2. Dr. Zakir Hussain was then the Vice Chancellor of Jamia Millia Islamia, and later became Vice President (1962-67) and then President of India (1967-69).

3. The title 'Sayyid' indicates a descendant of the Prophet Muhammad (S). (S) is the abbreviation of the preferred eulogy specific to the Prophet Muhammad (S), '*salla Allahu 'alayhi wa-sallam',* meaning 'May peace and blessings be upon him'.

After working for some time, I realized that it was not easy to accomplish the goal that I had in mind. Newspapers had become industries owned by the wealthy, hiring editors to write whatever they wished them to write in order to advance their own interests and pander to the political leaders they had selected. I had gone to Lahore with great hopes, but the state of journalism there led me to return to Delhi within a year.

On my return I met with Dr. Zakir Hussain. After listening to my story he realized that I was very discouraged, and tried to cheer me up and give me hope. He said that he was going to Bombay (now Mumbai) and would talk to Mr. Haris, the owner of the *Ajmal* newspaper and Mr. 'Abdullah Yusuf 'Ali, the editor of the paper *The Bombay Chronicle*, about me. Although hopeful that something would materialize, he pointed out, "Your desire to be a journalist and your enthusiasm for being of service through journalism can also be satisfied by being a teacher. As a journalist you will be dealing with personalities that have already been formed. You will then try to influence the direction a person takes and thereby inculcate good values in them. As a teacher you will be working with children whose personalities are still forming. You will have to understand the direction in which a child's personality is developing, assess their potential for growth, and then you will have to work with the child to take him or her to a level of excellence. You will have to direct the child's capacity for decision-making and action, and develop character that is strong and not fragmented, in the light of true principles. To do this you will have to fill your heart with passion and enthusiasm, so that with the warmth of that passion you can endow your students' character with integrity and dignity. This work is neither easy, nor is it a privilege that is bestowed upon everyone. In my view, developing the character of children and young people is the greatest source of pride and honor in life."

Dr. Zakir Hussain told me that at this time Jamia was celebrating its silver jubilee, and the achievements of the last twenty-five years were to be presented to the nation. "Teachers are working day and night to do this – it is your duty to help out as a volunteer!" When I immediately agreed to do so, he was very pleased and wrote a letter to Mr. 'Ateeq Ahmad who was in charge of the Jamia School in those days. I took the letter to Mr. 'Ateeq who was very happy with the letter and his meeting with me. He promptly appointed me to the post of teacher and tutor.

Jamia's jubilee celebrations went off beautifully and, shortly after this, India went through partition. I had to postpone my plan to work for the newspapers in Bombay. I focused on my work in Jamia and met very little with Dr. Zakir Hussain and the others who were in charge. One day however, I happened to meet Dr. Zakir Hussain by chance. Smiling at me in his characteristic manner, he said, "I have not been meeting you but I have been meeting your work." As he walked away, he told me to come and see him in his office. I thought about how much Dr. Zakir Hussain had said in that one sentence. In accordance with his wishes, I went to his office and he called me in immediately. First he gave me feedback on the educational projects I had run for the jubilee celebrations. The way in which he spoke of their strengths and weaknesses showed that he had studied each aspect very carefully.

Then he smiled a little and said, "You must have thought that I had forgotten you, but I did not forget at all. I spoke to Mr. Haris and 'Abdullah Yusuf 'Ali about you. From my conversation with them I have gathered that journalism in Bombay is in the same state as it is in Lahore. Now you can decide. Mr. 'Ateeq says that you have a natural gift for teaching children and young people and that you do your work with a great deal of enthusiasm, care, and diligence. A course in teacher training would be good for you." When I agreed to get trained, Dr. Zakir Hussain wrote to Mr. 'Ibadurrahman Khan, who was Education Secretary in Uttar Pradesh, for my admission. Previously Mr. Khan had been the principal of Allahabad's famous teacher training college. This college was special because together with theoretical and practical training, it included training in the crafts. As was the case in Jamia, Mr. Khan had put together a team of sincere teachers like Khalil ur-Rabb, D. P. Maheshwari, and K. Srivastav for whom work was a form of worship and its own reward. At that point in time, and as a degree from Jamia was not officially recognized, it was difficult to gain admission to the college. I did manage to get temporary admission and six months passed. Fortunately, during this period the Principal R. K. Soor was impressed with my performance and the manner in which I conducted myself. He authorized my admission by obtaining special permission from the Academic Council of the Allahabad University.

On returning to Jamia after having completed my training with distinction, Professor Mujib, the Vice-Chancellor of Jamia, appointed me to the position of Lecturer in the Teacher Training College. Shortly afterwards he put me in charge of the Primary School. The

Primary School was considered one of the most important educational departments of Jamia, because the school was the laboratory in which Dr. Zakir Hussain and his associates experimented with different pedagogies. In addition to incorporating the methodologies used in other countries, new methods of education were constantly being developed and experimentally implemented – which established Jamia Millia Islamia as an exemplary school. At this point, to be put in charge of this Primary School instead of being appointed a lecturer at the college was a great honor.

In India, there was on one hand the Dar ul-'Ulum Deoband that offered Muslims an education in traditional subjects, and on the other, the Aligarh Muslim University where students received a modern education. There was a need for a school that brought together the traditional and the modern in a harmonious blend, so Jamia Millia Islamia was founded to address this need. Every effort was made in Jamia to safeguard the blend of the modern with the traditional. Dr. Zakir Hussain, Dr. Sayyid 'Abid Hussain, Professor Muhammad Mujib, Professor E. J. Kallatt, Professor Muhammad Sarwar, Maulana Aslam Jairajpuri and Khwaja 'Abdul Hayy Faruqi were exemplary personalities. Although the Jamia had the word Islamia attached to it, there was no trace of any kind of prejudice or bias. Teachers from every school of thought were to be found there. Discussions were frank and open and every effort was made to understand the others' point of view. At times the discussions became animated, but they never became unpleasant nor had any adverse effect on relationships.

*

In those days, young people were very excited about Freud's theories. His concept of the unconscious and the sexual interpretation of human behavior had sent shock waves throughout the modern world. According to his theory, the cause of neuroses in human beings is the repression of desire. In his view, the reason for stress and mental illness is that human beings hide their desires from themselves. Since society, religion, morality, and tradition posed barriers to fulfilling their desires, young people had interpreted for themselves that these barriers were unnatural, authoritarian, and had no sound basis for existence. They thought that to achieve happiness it was necessary to be free of all the norms and laws governing social interaction.

There were also many young people who were not in complete agreement with Freud's views, and I was one of them. We felt that the conclusions that Freud had drawn from his study of mentally unstable people could not be applied to balanced, normal human beings. We also thought that the limits Freud had placed on the states of the human psyche were debatable. His contention that sexual desire or social convention and its pressures motivate every human action also did not appear to be true. In Islamic history, we have examples of prophets, saints, and holy people who joyfully performed outstanding feats that had nothing to do with social convention or traditions. Whatever they did was done voluntarily and for altruistic purposes.

At the time, communism and socialism were also very popular among students. Like other students, I too was impressed by the theory that economics was the fundamental determinant of human life, and believed a society could not sustain itself unless it was built on strong economic foundations. The fact that this theory had brought about a revolution in Russia was also very impressive. Their belief that human beings should live for an ideology, and should be willing to make sacrifices, to suffer and even die for their cause, was very appealing. In this spirit, the students often recited the following couplet:

Loyalty matched by constancy is the essence of belief
If he dies loyal to his idols, bury the Brahmin in the Ka'ba

At this time, Maulana 'Ubaidullah Sindhi was an honorary professor at the Jamia. Maulana was impressed by the Russian revolution because he had witnessed the inspiring effects of the revolution with his own eyes. He had wanted to meet Lenin, but in those days Lenin was very ill and they never met. At the same time, he was not disillusioned with Islam. His company and his conversation mitigated the effect communism was increasingly having on us. Maulana said, "Most Western schools of thought consider human beings to be material animals. They believe that the source of all human behavior is the body and nothing else. They ignore the spiritual and moral aspects. In their view, religion is an opiate, given by the feudal and capitalist class to the people to prevent them from engaging in class warfare. We do not deny the importance of economic factors, but we do not accept that their effects are inevitable and pre-determined or that this is the only determinant and there are no others. If we strengthen our belief in Islam, understand its principles in the way that the Prophet (S) explained them, and then adopt modern modes of production, Islam will not be adversely affected nor will we become socialists like the Russians." Maulana thought that the greatest flaw in the thinking of socialists was that they limited human needs to the need for food, clothing, and sex, while completely disregarding the spiritual and moral aspects of human existence. He said, "We accept the economic program of the socialists, but until this includes a belief in God, human beings cannot find ultimate fulfillment. A complete system for human life is one that ignores neither the material nor the spiritual needs of human beings."

My interaction with teachers from different schools of thought at Jamia began to make me doubt my traditional beliefs and views. The views of E. J. Kallat, a Christian professor of English at Jamia, intensified my doubts and uncertainties. He had an in-depth knowledge of English literature and the Bible, and was also in charge of sports. As I represented the University in every game and sport and was the captain of the hockey team, I interacted with him frequently. I often went to his house and asked searching questions about Christianity, which he answered with clarity, often quoting from the Bible. Due to the time I spent with Professor Kallat, I was given the opportunity to acquire a deep understanding of Christianity. My desire to do a comparative study of religions was also a result of our interaction. Professor Kallat maintained that the purpose of a college education was for us to examine all our beliefs and our religion and to re-think what it meant to be a Muslim. I took this so much to heart that my traditional faith was shaken. I began to look at everything with doubt and suspicion. I wanted to compare the beliefs of my religion with other religions and that made me to want to study further.

I had been fond of philosophy from the beginning, but among the many subjects offered at Jamia, philosophy was not among them. This was despite the presence of Dr. Sayyid 'Abid Hussain among the Jamia staff, who had received an excellent education in philosophy in Germany and who had studied the German philosopher Immanuel Kant in depth. To fulfill my desire to study philosophy, I asked Dr. Hussain, who used to teach Urdu at the college, to tutor me. There were some fundamental questions that I had been asking since I was a child that I had great hopes of answering through study. He happily agreed and under his guidance, I was able to make an in-depth study of Islamic and European philosophy.

One of the fundamental questions philosophers ask is, "What is the real essence of the universe?" or "What is the organizing principle behind the order evident in the universe?" My studies revealed that when the Greeks reflected on these questions, different philosophers came up with different answers. Some said water; some said fire; and some said that it was the interaction between love and strife that resulted in the material world. In time, philosophical thought became more refined and Pythagoras declared that number was the essence of the universe. The great philosophers Socrates, Plato, and Aristotle came to the conclusion that only the intellect existed in reality, and everything else was a manifestation of the intellect at different levels. This theory dominated the thought of the following generations to such an extent that for centuries Greek philosophy reigned uncontested in the West.

This conception gained such popularity that most thinkers adopted the belief that the intellect was the essence of the universe and the criterion for truth. Aristotle maintained that God was pure intellect and His own cause. As a result, most philosophers were not comfortable venturing beyond space, time, and matter, dismissing as delusional the views of those who tried to look further. In reality, these philosophers were fearful that if they were to go beyond the world of the limited intellect, they would fall into a limitless vacuum. It appeared that these great philosophers were caught in the delusion that it was through the intellect and the material world that the best of worlds for human beings could be created. There was no need to turn to the prophets for guidance.

In ancient and modern philosophy many great thinkers have tried to prove the limitations of rationality. In particular, Kant played a major role in the deconstruction of logic and rationalism. Kant demonstrated that it is not possible to solve metaphysical problems through the use of logical reasoning, for it cannot shed light on the beginning and the end of the universe nor can it prove the existence of God. He maintained that the power of the human mind and senses is limited, and hence people cannot reach the sublime heights that are required to know the secrets of the universe, human beings, and God. Kant, to a great extent, tried to counter the trend towards an exaggerated rationalism that inclined towards skepticism – a kind of rationalism that had begun with Francis Bacon and René Descartes, and had reached its zenith with Descartes' skepticism. Kant took the stance of denying the decisive role of the intellect in solving metaphysical problems, for there was no other path he could have taken.

At the same time Charles Darwin mounted a fresh attack on religion, which had initially been led by Voltaire and his followers. Arthur Schopenhauer attacked and ridiculed his successful opponents and was compelled to conclude after studying Kant that ambiguity can be meaningful. As a result, mechanical materialism started to regain strength. Fichte, Schelling, and Hegel took advantage of this attack and paved the way for metaphysics to re-enter the arena, spinning conceptual webs from its splendid warp and woof. Their fundamental premise was that metaphysical questions could be resolved through the intellect, and as in science, hypotheses could be proved or disproved. As materialism, science, and experimentalism had become dominant once again, those who wished to understand reality in the broadest sense reacted against this. This reaction took the shape of movements such as existentialism, logical positivism, and pragmatism.

Eminent philosophers such as Søren Kierkegard, William James, and Alfred North Whitehead produced strong arguments to show that logical arguments, rationality, and traditional materialism were intellectually unacceptable and insufficient for comprehending the infinite aspects of existence. I was quite impressed in particular by the works of the two philosophers, Kierkegard and Henri Bergson. In despair, Kierkegard took refuge in faith by choosing religion over ethics towards the end of his life. In other words, he took a leap of faith and was possessed by an intense desire to establish a connection with God. Even though he had handed himself over to God, it did not give him peace. A study of his life reveals that he failed to understand the will of his Creator. In the final analysis, despite his efforts and struggle, he died leaving his quest for Truth incomplete.

Bergson tried to counteract the excesses of the worshippers of mechanical materialism. According to Bergson, realities could only be known through intuition, claiming that the mystics of every religion had tried to reach Reality through true intuition. There is no doubt that, through Bergson, I gained many insights, yet I still could not see any meaning in Bergson's theory of the flow of life, because in my view, existence cannot be seen as purposeless. In Bergson's view life is pre-determined and there is no room for free will. Clearly, without free will there can be no concept of morality.

When I tried to understand the reality of life through philosophy and studied and reflected on the efforts, theories, and counter-theories of philosophers, I came to the conclusion that philosophers had no source of knowledge other than the intellect. Intellectual theories have always been subject to mutual contradiction and change, therefore there is no absolute, and in this situation, there can be no question of conceiving of the existence of God.

How could I have understood whether you exist or don't?
Mutually contradictory were the theories of the intellect.
Intellect is not far from the door,
But being in the Presence is not its destiny.
Ask God for a heart that can see,
The light of the eye is not to be mistaken
for the light of the heart.
Transcend the intellect,
It illuminates the path – it is not the final destination.

All my efforts gave no answers to my questions. Philosophy took me to the door of Reality but could not show me in. Disappointed, I turned my attention to science.

*

When the age of science and philosophy began in Europe, the discoveries of eminent scientists such as Copernicus, Kepler, Galileo, and Bruno were in conflict with the teachings of the Bible and the Church of Rome. The religious opposed the supporters of science, and the opposition acquired more intensity as time went on, with the Inquisition, in the main, responsible for fuelling the conflict. At its altar, the Popes sacrificed hundreds of scientists in the medieval age for having committed the sin of scientific discovery. As a result, a battle ensued between science and Christianity that alienated the religion from itself. By sacrificing his life, Bruno had underscored this declaration of war. Sometimes I think if the priests had not opposed science indiscriminately, the world may have been a very different place today. Perhaps we would not have had the kind of bloodshed that has taken place, and we might have been a thousand years ahead of where we are now in terms of culture and civilization.

Science abandoned ideological thinking and took the empirical path. Unfortunately, at the very beginning of its quest it declared that science had nothing to do with the higher human values. The goal of science was not to discover the reality behind the manifestations of nature, but to discover the relationship and interaction between different things in the universe, and to find out the properties of things so they could be more fully utilized. I therefore doubted that science could help to resolve my dilemma, but I continued my study nevertheless.

The present age of rationality is represented by the last three hundred years in the West. The age has been marked by tremendous achievements in the material world and it helped to purify religion of many superstitions. However, the focus on mastering the physical world has made human beings oblivious to the inner realities, leading not only to a denial of God, but also a denial of the self and metaphysical realities. The intellect and the material world were thought to be the only realities: life, thought, will, and perception, everything was in the grips of this empirical view. My own generation, and in particular the youth, began to consider the concept of a creator of the universe as unnecessary. The collective view was that the state of the universe is determined every moment, and accordingly keeps reshaping itself. Nature could sustain itself without the interference of deities. Therefore the concept of a Creator as an intelligent force was meaningless.

Prominent scientists made arrogant claims, uttering profanities such as "We have thanked God for his temporary services and exiled him." Aldous Huxley said, "Matter and the laws governing matter have proved belief in creation and spirit to be false." Many of those in my age group began to doubt religion and became even more deeply impressed with science. In our youth, we learned that something that had produced such astonishing miracles had declared God and religion to be false, so there was little left to believe in. Lack of interest in religion became fashionable and essential to being considered open-minded. "Disbelief took the place of belief, intellect of revelation, the earth of the sky, action [the place] of worship." (Parkinson)

Simultaneously however, and by a strange coincidence, Einstein's theory of relativity and Heisenberg's theory of uncertainty led to an extraordinary revolution in the world of cause and effect. In this way the spell of the materialists and atheists, which had been cast in an authoritarian manner from the hard facts of science, was broken. Through their research and discoveries, scientists themselves had deconstructed materialism forever. Materialism, born of physics, and the inevitable result of scientific postulates, is gradually disappearing and some of today's scientists have started giving importance to the self, the spirit, and the intellect. As Bertrand Russell has said, more than philosophy, it was Einstein's theory of relativity that made matter as the essence of the universe disappear. Space and time were no longer thought of as constant, infinite, and unchanging, nor was matter thought of as a permanent unchanging substance. Einstein said that without religion science is lame and without science religion is blind.

The direction science took was itself responsible for turning it towards idealism, spirituality, and religion. In the same way that Descartes had to rely on God and his attributes to move beyond his mind and ego, the scientist James Jean came to the conclusion that the reason for the similarity in the perceptions of our egos and minds had to lie outside the mind. To think that this feat was a product of our minds is illogical. The only acceptable explanation is that there is an eternal, universal mind.

In philosophy, George Berkeley had already paved the way by coming up with the concept of an eternal spirit. The conclusion James Jean had come to through a purely scientific process was the same that Berkeley had arrived at by following a purely philosophical path. Even the well-respected Sir Arthur Stanley Eddington thought the theory was in harmony with science and it was perfectly rational to extrapolate the existence of a universal mind. I began to wonder how James Jean's universal mind could be anything other than what, in religion, is known as God. Despite this my heart was still not at peace. The study of science made it manifestly clear that one would not have access to a realm other than the observable world, irrespective of whether one approached the subject as a philosopher or as a scientist. The status of both logic and science appeared to be dubious. Even after all this study, I found no peace or contentment. Impressed by different theories and movements, I had tried to quench my thirst, mistaking a dazzling mirage for water, and I was still thirsty.

He who captured the rays of the sun
Could not travel through the dark night of life,
He who sought to know the paths of the stars
Could not traverse the world of his own thoughts.

One of the problems was that the conclusions reached through my study and inquiry conflicted with each other. My mind allowed an idea to enter, and at another point, when an entirely different idea knocked at its door, it had no objection to letting that in also. As a result there was no continuity of my thought and no peace of mind. My life had become a victim of this mental fragmentation and I suffered constantly from restlessness and frustration. I did not have complete faith, nor could I totally deny God. My heart and mind were perpetually in the grip of doubt and confusion. Yet it had become fairly clear to me that although the mind could shed some light along the way, it was not the final destination. As Maulana Abu'l-

Kalam Azad has said, philosophy opens the door of doubt but then cannot close it. Science can offer proof but not faith. Religion offers us faith, and to live fully we need not just proven truths, but also faith. After my disappointment with science, spiritual insight and intuition were my last hope. Perhaps by putting aside the mind, I could jump into this limitless ocean and reach the depths of reality.

I have unraveled the complexities of the mind
O my Lord, bless me with passion!

It was in my nature to want whatever conclusion I reached to be based on my personal experience. I wanted to develop a deep and harmonious relationship with this remarkable universe and with primordial Reality.

*

Most European and American philosophers mention spiritual intuition in some form or another and yet, due to the dominance of rationality, it has never gained popularity. Although many philosophers remained focused on the properties of space, time, and matter, the rationality of Socrates and Plato was not without the concept of something that transcended the mind. Here too I found the exalted concept of primordial love. Socrates admitted that at critical points in his life he had received guidance from intuition that had nothing to do with logic or analysis. Those who have had religious or gnostic experiences have, since ancient times, maintained that this way of knowing primordial Reality has been widely experienced by human beings.

I began to think that the experiences related with complete sanity by particular individuals from different nations and communities could not be dismissed as illusory or fraudulent. These people maintained that apart from sensory perception and rationality, there were intuitive ways of knowing Reality. Human beings have not only been endowed with the five basic senses, but also with subtle inner faculties that can reveal aspects of Reality that are not accessible to ordinary perception or the mind. Simply because spiritual intuition is inexpressible, and language has its limitations and falls short of expressing intuition's true nature, does not mean that intuition is a product of whim and fancy or is unreliable. There could be no doubt that Reality could not be captured in words, bound by logic, or limited by any single concept.

In addition to philosophy and science I studied the efforts of psychiatrists and psychologists, and took heart from this work. At first these experts considered extraordinary states of mind, inner experiences, and observations as signs of disease, and used medicine to suppress them, but after some time the situation changed. The psychiatrist C.G. Jung claimed that spiritual and intuitive knowledge were beyond psychology and could not be encompassed by it. In his search, he reached such vistas of human nature that his research brought him close to invisible phenomena and spirituality. Through this work, spirituality, which had lost its importance due to the scientific and industrial revolutions, once again became part of mainstream discourse. In the public realm, in academic institutions, and especially among psychiatrists and psychologists, the value and significance of spiritual and intuitive experience increased as people became more interested in spiritual practices and meditation. An attempt was made to present spirituality's positive elements in a new scientific language. Psychologists acknowledged that in the treatment of patients, spiritual experience was not simply a figment of the imagination, but was based on personal experience and had its own significance in the psychological make-up of the person. Jung's work established the spiritual dimension of an individual's experience as an important aspect of life - an aspect that makes life meaningful. Through his work psychologists came to accept that the spiritual aspect could not be ignored in the treatment of mental illness.

Imam Al-Ghazali (r) (d. 1111) is unique among theologians. On the one hand, like Kant, he shattered narrow-minded logic, and, on the other, for spiritual fulfillment he adopted the Sufi path at a time when his fame was at its height. After abandoning writing, teaching, and status, he traveled alone, attesting that the period in which he had been teaching had been a time of misfortune. He finally declared that unless knowledge was weighed in the scale of spiritual intuition, it was not possible to have access to true knowledge and Reality, that the path to Reality must pass through the valley of mysticism, and that spiritual intuition transcends logic and that this intuition is the true fountainhead of religion. According to Imam Al-Ghazali (r), the levels of intellect do not end with ordinary people and philosophers. There is another level, which he calls the prophetic intellect. In the final analysis Imam Al-Ghazali (r) took refuge in Sufi intuition and experience, acknowledging that the Sufis were the real guides to Reality. In intuition he found a basis for religion other than rationality. In this way he freed religion from science and metaphysics.

Finally, like Imam Al-Ghazali (r), I had no option except to turn my attention to spiritual intuition and work on developing it. This was not something theoretical because it calls for rigorous contemplative practices. I made every effort and tried to adopt whatever method appeared appropriate. If someone said that you had to become a *brahamachari* (a celibate) to reach Brahma, I did it. Before I met Hazrat, while living a celibate life, I went and met a Swami in Allahabad, Param Hans, and learned Vedanta and yoga from him.[4] Then I went and took a holy bath at Tribeni where the Ganges and Yamuna rivers meet, chanted the name of Ram, and was drawn to the devotional path of Bhakti. The *Bhagavad Gita* pleased me so much that I read it countless times and memorized many of its dialogues – it is without parallel in how it unifies the realities of mysticism with action.

In this book, the war of the battlefield and the war against the ego have been infused with the philosophy of the unity of God in such a way that it removes many of the defects of a mysticism that renounces the world. In spite of all my struggle and ascetic practices, my heart still found no peace and Reality eluded me. I had reservations about the yogi claim *aham brahmasam* (I am God, there is no difference between God and I) and that certain techniques if adopted and practiced with ascetic rigor were sufficient to lead the seeker to Reality. Difficult ascetic practices revealed such remarkable spiritual powers of the ego to the yogis that they mistakenly proclaimed that there was no need for guidance from prophets. As a result they were deflected from the path of Truth. It is also a fact that Hinduism and Buddhism both teach renunciation of the world and consider *sadhus* and *bhikshus* (Hindu and Buddhist monks) to be superior to other human beings. To renounce the world and live the life of an ascetic was thought to be a highly desirable goal for all human beings.

As far as Muslim Sufis and holy people are concerned, there was hardly an important shrine where I did not pay homage. I went to Lahore, Lucknow, Allahabad, Aurangabad, Trichinapali, and Nag Patam in the south - the resting places of the great Muslim saints. When living in Lahore I had the opportunity of visiting the shrines of these holy people, and because I knew Hazrat 'Ali Hujwiri's (r) book, *Kashf ul-mahjub* (*Unveiling the Veiled*) I spent much time at his shrine and undertook a forty-day retreat there. I also spent time in Dankaur in Uttar Pradesh, with Hazrat Lutfullah Shah (r) who belonged to the Chishti-Nizami Sufi order (*tariqa*) and was one of the

4. Param Hans, literally meaning great swan, is an enlightened person who attains the highest stage of awareness (Skt. *sahaj samadhi*).

great Sufis of his time. Under his instruction I performed a recollection of God (*dhikr*) that is repeated aloud thousands of times while holding the breath. Yet, after all the hard work and all the difficult ascetic practices I still could not find the peace of heart and the contentment I had wanted. The thirst and the longing stayed with me. I met Sufis, but they were those who were living in solitude, practicing a form of mysticism that called for the renunciation of life. Their practices were full of actions that were outside the Prophetic sunna, so they did not appeal to me.[5]

As a result of my participation in outdoor games in my student days, I was fit and although the rigorous practices I performed in this pursuit of Truth did not daunt me, and I spared no effort whatsoever, my goal eluded me. The more effort I made, the further I seemed to be from my goal. Sometimes I tried to reach the secrets of life through the intellect, and at other times I would get fed up and jump into the ocean of mystical experience. Until the end I was caught in this dilemma:

The nights of my existence, I spent in deep quandary
Now the longing and the music of Rumi,
Now the intellectual subtleties of Razi [6]

There is no denying that my efforts were not wasted because I did acquire certain spiritual powers. I understood many things about spiritual intuition and spiritual states but I could not get to Reality. If some door of spirituality opened, it was tantamount to its not having actually been opened.

The truth is that when divine grace is with you and destiny is kind to you, someone or another appears, like Khidr (s), to guide you.[7] So, when I was in this state of despair and lost in the narrow alleyways of my thoughts, I saw a glimmer of hope. Mr. Rauz ur-Rahman advised me to meet the Sufi shaykh, Hazrat Maulvi Mu-

5. To follow the sunna is to emulate the way, or tradition of the Prophet (S) and lead a life that is pleasing to God. The basic source of the sunna is the hadith, or recorded sayings and actions of the Prophet Muhammad (S).
6. Maulana Jalaluddin Rumi (d. 1273) is a well-known poet and mystic; Fakhruddin Razi (d. 1209) is a well-known religious scholar.
7. Khidr is the 'green man', the unnamed guide to Moses referred to in the Holy Qur'an (18:60-82). There are differences of opinion as to whether he is a prophet or not. The abbreviation of '*alayhi as-salam*, abbreviated (s), means 'may peace be upon him/her/them' and is used as an honorific for prophets other than Muhammad (S) and for angels.

hammad Sa'id Khan Sahib (r).[8] After spending precious years of my life in this quest for Truth, I had become exhausted and disheartened. Dissatisfaction had created a bitterness in my life that is not so difficult to imagine, yet my passion had not completely left me. So half-heartedly, with conflicting feelings of fear and enthusiasm, restlessness and calm, and experiencing feelings of both doubt and certainty, I entered Hazrat's presence.

Hazrat spared no effort in my training and education. I was like an uncut stone in the hands of a jeweller. He led me to the limitless ocean of knowledge and Truth. Hazrat's sacred being was the repository of this ocean; his company, attention and bounty transformed me. The veils were lifted from my eyes and then I understood what was true. My greatest desire was at last fulfilled.

*

The greatest difficulty on this path is that the seeker's mind has been conditioned over the years by the environment, living conditions, and education. The seeker develops a certain frame of reference where thoughts gradually acquire the status of beliefs. It therefore becomes very difficult for the mind to accept anything new. All kinds of doubts and suspicions arise and the mind interprets anything that is new according to its own frame of reference. I too found myself in this predicament because my mind had developed along certain lines. There is a saying that knowledge can itself become the greatest veil. Despite my desire to follow the path, I found myself resisting what did not conform to my expectations.

It was much like someone wanting to cross a whirlpool but getting caught in it, spinning around and around. My mind interpreted what was new in a manner that made me averse to it, or if not averse, I found it difficult to be consistent in my thinking. Hazrat was aware of this tendency of mine and started my training on the condition that for a period of one-and-a-half to two years I did the practices I was given without questioning. After I started my training with Hazrat, as could be expected, all kinds of doubts and suspicions arose in my mind and it began to churn out its own interpretations of my experience. For example, spiritual attention/transmission (*tawajjuh*) and autosuggestion appeared to be the same. I began to think there

8. *Sahib* is an Indian term of respect (lit. Ar. friend) which follows an individual's name. See the Author's Preface for a full description of his first meeting with Hazrat Maulvi Muhammad Sa'id Khan Sahib (r).

was no difference in what the Sufis call meditation (*muraqaba*) and what the Hindus call the experience of a unitary consciousness (*samadhi*). The science of the chakras in yoga and the subtle centers of consciousness (*lata'if*) in Sufism also appeared to be very similar. Therefore, I came to the conclusion that the practices were not going to be of much use to me. However, despite all these doubts, and since I had made a promise to Hazrat, I made every effort to perform the practices in accordance with his instructions.

The result was that gradually the hold of the mind's conditioning began to loosen and the effects of Hazrat's guidance started to become visible. Just like a blind person whose vision has been restored can see what the seeker could not have seen in the previous state, the veils lifted and I could see what had not been visible and was beyond the reach of the mind. Hazrat's blessings released me from the confines of rationality and led me to the vast ocean of spiritual insight. My entire perspective changed and the knots the mind had tied itself up in, began to slowly unravel.

A secret philosophers could not unravel, intellectuals
could not fathom,
In a few gestures a pious man wrapped in a mantle
revealed to me.

My most important realization was that the knowledge of God's prophets (s) is absolute in its finality. A mind trapped in materialism cannot develop the requisite faith in God. If the mind could grasp the depths of the human self then it could have acquired knowledge of the self and with it, the knowledge of God.

It also became clear to me that spiritual practices and austerities lead to certainty when they are associated with what has been confirmed by the prophets (s) who preach on God's behalf. When spiritual practices and austerities are practiced without following the prophets (s), the cleansing of the self (*nafs*) that takes place leaves room for error. This purification of the self deludes the seeker into making gods out of mental projections so that the seeker feels no need for guidance from the prophets (s). The purification of the self is connected to the purification of the heart. The heart is the door through which guidance enters, and guidance comes from following the prophets (s).

It also became clear to me that within the human body it was not only the mind but also the heart that was a locus of knowledge. Other than the five senses, the Holy Qur'an also recognizes the heart as a source of divine knowledge. The Holy Qur'an has revealed the reality that the heart does not use logic, for it has the capacity to envision. The heart's vision has nothing to do with the five outer senses. What the inner eye sees is to be considered no less reliable than what is seen by the physical eye. This inner vision is what leads us to Reality. It transcends reason and is the true fountainhead of religion. It is the purpose of living itself. Its flow is determined not by external acts, but by an inner inclination.

I also realized that the inner and outer worlds are not unconnected. The inner world of the individual (*anfus*) and the outer world (*afaq*) are two aspects of the same Reality. The Holy Qur'an does not denigrate the material realm and enjoin its renunciation; instead it presents the outer and inner realms as aspects of the same Reality. This is one of the Holy Qur'an's remarkable feats. Many ancient religions and civilizations were unsuccessful and obstacles to human perfection and excellence because they separated the inner and outer realities and focused on one to the exclusion of the other.

*

As I have said previously, my plan to become a journalist never materialized. Today when I turn and look back on my life, I feel this was better for me and I did not lose out in any way. This was the gift of a great man, Dr Zakir Hussain. Due to his far-sightedness and knowledge of human character, he made his humble student who wanted to be a journalist into a teacher, and put him on the path to success. A good teacher remains at all times and in all places a teacher to the very last because a teacher's work is never done. Sometimes a teacher is engaged in improving the lives of children, at others in guiding the youth so they can realize their potential, and at other times, inspiring adults and older people to be proactive. After retirement, I was hardly free of the task of educating personalities in the process of formation. I saw before me a vast field of work that was greater than the task I had previously undertaken - the character building of adults. I then directed all my attention towards the training and character building of young people and adults. To do this work I had to make myself worthy of it by putting myself through fire. Only after this could I start working in a disciplined and systematic way. Today it has been nearly twenty-five years since I started the work of the Institute of Search for Truth and I will continue with this work until my last breath.

If Dr. Zakir Hussain were alive, he would have praised my humble effort and would have been happy. He would have seen it as part of the Jamia's extensive educational program of *Bayt ul-Hikmat* (House of Wisdom). Dr. Zakir Hussain was right when he said that character building is perhaps the most difficult and the most important of the tasks undertaken by human beings in their individual and collective capacity. The path to this building seems to be the integration of the different, and at times conflicting, skills and capacities that nature has bestowed upon human beings. An individual's unformed morals and instincts need to be woven into an integrated personality. This personality needs to be engaged in the service of higher human values and taken to the exalted status of a moral personality. Probably the most precious pearl in the treasures of the universe is a moral human being. Even the angels are envious of such a being. The Creator of the Universe takes pride in this marvel.

Azad Rasool, Delhi
September 2006

Chapter One

The Life and Times of Hazrat Maulvi Muhammad Sa'id Khan

Hazrat Maulvi Sa'id Khan Sahib (r) was born in the home of his maternal grandparents in Chattapur Sarai, in the District Azamgarh, Uttar Pradesh, in November 1907 (1325 Hijri), during the last ten days of Ramadan. Hazrat was originally from Nonari, a well-known area near the town of Sarai Mir in Azamgarh, but he subsequently moved to Mangarawan, another town in the same region. Hazrat owned a house and some agricultural land in Mangarawan, but because of his job he stayed in Azamgarh where he lived in a rented house behind the Jami' Masjid. His father, 'Abdussattar Sahib, supervised the tilling of the land in Mangarawan and after he passed away, Hazrat's son took over this responsibility.

Hazrat's father, 'Abdussattar Sahib, had himself memorized the Holy Qur'an and was therefore very keen that Hazrat should also memorize the Holy Qur'an before going on to further education. With this in mind, he sent Hazrat to a local school. Hazrat had excellent powers of retention and so was able to commit the Holy Qur'an to memory in a very short period of time. He used to say that memorization of the Holy Qur'an facilitates the acquisition of all other kinds of knowledge. After he had completely memorized the Holy Qur'an Hazrat studied it once again with a view to perfecting his pronunciation. He studied with Hafiz 'Abdurrahman, a prominent Qur'an reciter who had written a booklet called *Mutashabihat-i Qur'an.*[1] Hazrat had been very keen to have the booklet published, but his desire was not fulfilled.

After memorizing the Holy Qur'an Hazrat studied elementary Arabic and Persian in the town of Bakhra near Nonari. He was then admitted to the Madrasa Zia ul-'Ulum in Kanpur where he completed his education within a year (1925-1926). At this point, a few of his relatives made some derogatory remarks about him having become 'eligible to collect charity'. Hazrat felt so mortified by these comments that he studied the matriculation curriculum on his own and passed the exam without hiring a tutor. While Hazrat was study-

1. *Hafiz* is the title given to someone who has memorized the Qur'an. Common mistakes made in Qur'anic recitation and ambiguous verses in the Qur'an are called *mutashabihat.*

ing in Kanpur, his maternal uncle used to send him fifteen rupees a month. At one point however, a misunderstanding occurred between Hazrat and his uncle and Hazrat's sense of self-respect did not allow him write to his uncle for money again. He managed to survive somehow, even resorting to living on barley for some time. It was quite awhile before the fifteen-rupee money order arrived again, and Hazrat did not go home in the interim.

In 1928 Hazrat had the opportunity to work as a teacher and tutor at the Madrasa Muhammadiyya in Allahabad. For ten years, Hazrat served in this institution with enthusiasm and zeal, and during this time Hazrat also passed his Greek medical exams. Hazrat was very strict about matters relating to adherence to the sunna, which was probably due to his affinity to the Mujaddidi Sufi order founded by Ahmad Sirhindi (r). He put great emphasis on building the character of individual students and felt greatly distressed when he perceived the slightest deviation from the sunna in his students' attitudes or actions. He did his utmost to ensure that his students did not disregard even the most minor injunction. Hazrat worked tirelessly to raise the standard of the teaching at the school and was also in charge of the school's hostel, always taking care to speak and spend time with the students, fulfilling his duties with the greatest sincerity. Once in Delhi, I happened to meet Mr. Muhammad Miyan, the administrator of the Madrasa Muhammadiyya. Muhammad Miyan told me that during Hazrat's ten years at the Madrasa, not only had Hazrat been an exemplary teacher, but had also been a highly regarded member of staff in charge of much of the administration at the school.

After serving at the Madrasa for ten years Hazrat decided to return home. He used to say that he had achieved nothing in those ten years. However, in Allahabad he did have the opportunity to observe closely communist leaders like Dr. Ashraf, Sajjad Zaheer and others – men whose entire wardrobe consisted of two *kurtas* (shirts) and two *pajamas* (pants). Hazrat was impressed with the way these people endured adversity and were willing to make all kinds of sacrifices for their cause. He was also distressed about his own inertia regarding a subject close to his heart – his religion. He made a firm decision to do something about it no matter what sacrifices it involved.

On his return from Allahabad, Hazrat taught for a while. In 1941, a vacancy for an Arabic teacher came up in the Shibli School in Azamgarh. Hazrat applied for this post, as did Maulvi 'Abdussalam, and since they were both from the same background, both were selected to teach at the school. Hazrat began teaching Arabic and Urdu and worked under three different principals in his time there. During this time a vacancy arose in the Madrasa-yi 'Alia in Calcutta (now Kolkata). Hazrat thought that if he took the job, he could live in Bandel and ensure that the Sufi lodge (*khanaqah*) there thrived. He could also pursue more easily his principal aim of promoting the Naqshbandi-Mujaddidi Sufi order. God had some other plans for him, however, and he did not succeed in moving to Calcutta. When he finally retired, after twenty-seven years of honorable and meritorious service, Hazrat felt once again that he should move to Bandel because it was centrally located and it would be easier for him to work for the order from there. With this aim in mind, Hazrat stayed in Bandel for a while, and during this time I was also fortunate to have the opportunity to stay in Bandel with my wife and children.

In Bandel, as part of his daily routine, he not only performed the daily practices but also spent some time studying the hadith and the Holy Qur'an. It was also usual for him to read a few pages of the *Maktubat*, the letters of Hazrat Shaykh Ahmad Faruqi Sirhindi (r). When he felt inspired and had the opportunity, Hazrat also wrote his own thoughts on paper. If some others were present he dictated his thoughts to them. There was always a steady stream of seekers visiting from all over the Subcontinent who participated in all the daily practices. When time allowed, Hazrat gave them the opportunity to talk to him. In those days Hazrat also used to go on tours to spread the work and practices of the order.

At the insistence of his son 'Azduddin Miyan, Hazrat moved to Aligarh for a while, and in those days, he also spent some time at my house in Delhi. After a few months however, Hazrat left to live in Azamgarh in a house he had previously rented, staying there until he passed away. During his last days Hazrat had given up going to the mosque because of intense soreness in his feet and offered most of his prayers at home. He did, however, continue to receive visitors who stayed at the nearby Jami' Masjid. During this time there was at least one gathering in his house, which enabled the visitors to discuss their personal matters and other affairs with him.

*

Having memorized the Holy Qur'an Hazrat had a deep knowledge of it and could recite it beautifully. When he recited the Holy Qur'an in Ramadan a state of spiritual ecstasy was created. Hazrat used to say that he always experienced at least one common error in the recitation when he recited the Holy Qur'an. One day when Hazrat was reciting, he experienced many errors. Hazrat ended his prayers hastily and then turned around to look behind him. It became apparent that a few youths in the last row had joined in without doing proper ablutions before prayer. They were asked to leave and then the errors did not occur again.

After Hazrat had joined the Naqshbandi-Mujaddidi order and completed the practices of all the other five different orders, his recitation of the Holy Qur'an was transformed. When Hazrat began reciting, the listeners did not feel any tiredness or weakness but instead experienced a sense of blissful exhilaration. The entire atmosphere was infused with spiritual rapture.

I was fortunate enough to have had several opportunities to hear him recite the Holy Qur'an. When Hazrat was in his hometown he went to the mosque to recite, and when traveling he led the special supererogatory prayers recited after the evening prayer during Ramadan (*tarawih*) in the house of one of his disciples. The house that had the most capacity for accommodating disciples was usually chosen. The evening prayer was always performed at home, followed by *tarawih* prayers. Since Hazrat's stay was usually short, he planned to complete the entire Qur'an in three to seven days. The amazing thing is that his followers did not find the prayers burdensome, for they felt neither sleepy nor tired. On one occasion, during the last or second-to-last night of Ramadan, at the insistence of his followers, Hazrat stood up to recite and completed the whole Qur'an in just two cycles (sing. *raka't*) of prayer. Everyone went into a state of spiritual ecstasy. The radiant splendors of the Holy Qur'an were visible for a long time, like pure and luminous waves. His followers continued to listen in a state of bliss in the sanctified surroundings.

*

In 1971 he went on pilgrimage via Basra, Najaf, Karbala, Kazimayn, Baghdad and Salman Pak before proceeding to the pilgrimage in Mecca and Medina. By 1972, Hazrat had performed the Hajj pilgrimage five times. Hazrat performed his first pilgrimage in 1949 when a friend, Mr. Muhammad Ya'qub, who had been planning to go for Hajj, put Hazrat's name in the Hajj ballot along with his own. Hazrat's name was drawn. I happened to be with Hazrat in Calcutta at the time and tried to have my name added to the list of pilgrims, but it was too late and I was unable to do so. Hazrat then made an unscheduled trip to Bombay where he met his father and son-in-law before setting off for the holy city of Mecca.

It was summer and the heat in Mecca was intense. Hazrat had said later that it had been a very difficult experience. He said that, "At one point I felt like I was losing consciousness and lay down in the shade of a bus. I thought my time had come but God had mercy on me. After awhile I recovered and was able to perform all the rituals of Hajj with ease."

In 1967, Hazrat decided to go for Hajj again. I also tried, thinking it would be very fortunate indeed if I were to have the honor of performing the pilgrimage with him, but my name was not drawn in the ballot. However, Hazrat told me to keep trying, and eventually Mr. Kamil Qidwai managed to get a special permit for me. We left by ship from Bombay and Hazrat told us to consider ourselves guests of Allah, and that as such, no words of complaint should pass our lips. Hazrat's wife, his son-in-law Izhar Bhai, and Ishaq Seth of Malegaon traveled with us. There were also some other people from the Naqshbandi order, as well as Ghulam Maula of Bangladesh. In Mecca, Hazrat met the central axial authority (*qutub-i madar*), who indicated to Hazrat that he had received his teaching from more than one master, which was true.[2] Hazrat had received most of his transmissions on the subtle centers of consciousness through Hakim Ahsan Miyan of Allahabad and had also received some transmissions from Jameel Miyan.

In Mecca, we stayed in the neighborhood of Jiad and entered the area of the Ka'ba through that side. We said our prayers in the corridor that had been built by the Turks and was directly in front of the black stone in the wall of the Ka'ba. Hazrat usually spent most of his time sitting in the sacred precincts of the Ka'ba and never tired of looking at it. He used to say that there are two forms of worship that cannot be performed anywhere else. The first one is looking at the Ka'ba, and the other is circumambulating it. During circumambulation Hazrat never appeared to be making an effort to kiss the black stone but just allowed himself to be carried forward by the crowd

---

2. There is the axial guide (*qutb-i irshad*), while his deputy is called the central axial authority (*qutb-i madar*). They say that the lower station of the axial guide is the shadow of the upper station, i.e., the central axial authority.

and we suddenly saw him near the black stone. Similarly, due to Hazrat's presence, the Hajj was made easy for us.

During that time, I asked Hazrat how one should go about seeking forgiveness for shortcomings in fulfilling our obligations towards our fellow human beings (*huquq al-'ibad*). Hazrat replied that all these obligations are forgiven during the night that is spent in Muzdalifa during Hajj. Hazrat said that just as staying in a place where the air is fresh and healthful can rejuvenate one, and give one a sense of well-being, Allah has made the atmosphere of these holy places soul-cleansing when one passes through them. All one's sins fall off like leaves from a tree and one becomes as pure as a new-born baby. Hazrat also told us that if someone should get lost in the crowd, he should not wander around in a panic but should sit quietly in one spot for a while, for when he gets up again he will find his tent nearby.

In Medina, we did our spiritual practices at the foot of the Prophet's (S) grave and also went to visit the tombs of the *ahl-i bayt* in Jannat al-Baqi as well as other shrines.[3] Hazrat said that it was preferable to recite the blessings on the Prophet (S) and his family (*salawat-i sharif*) at these places. He also said that it is of utmost importance to be extremely respectful and not guilty of the slightest breach of decorum in Medina. He added that if one lives long enough and has the financial wherewithal, one should make one trip to Medina solely for the purpose of visiting the Prophet's (S) shrine. Hazrat found it hard to leave the sanctuaries of Mecca and Medina. At the time of our departure, when Hazrat offered his last salutations and unwillingly bid farewell, he looked extremely dejected.

*

Hazrat was a scholar and as such had great respect for Muslim religious scholars and often sought meetings with them. In his youth he enjoyed attending religious sermons and also studied. He did not find peace or solace in these pursuits and continued to wander in search of the truth, saying, "I had some superstitious notions about Sufism, and couldn't see the truth shining brilliantly in front of me. I was in a state of despair. Islam was my heritage and I could not deny it, but I had a burning desire to find the truth." He wrote a letter to Hazrat Hamid Hasan 'Alawi (r) saying, "My faith is based on conformity, since I was born in a Muslim family and have been fol-

3. *Ahl-i bayt* - the family of the Prophet (S).

lowing in the footsteps of my ancestors. If that is not all there is to know and if there is something more, I entreat you to tell me."

In his reply, Hazrat Hamid Hasan 'Alawi (r) asked Hazrat to come to Allahabad to meet him. Hazrat had tried to go to Kohanda with Khan Sahib, but was unable to do so. Therefore, the first meeting between Hazrat and Hazrat Hamid Hasan 'Alawi (r) took place in Allahabad at the house of Mr. Ahmadullah. At first Mr. 'Abdul Jalil spoke to him, and then he recited the following verse from the Holy Qur'an (5:35): *Oh you who believe! Be mindful of your duty to Allah. Seek the means to come to Him and strive in His way in order that you may succeed.* Hazrat Maulvi Sa'id Khan Sahib (r) replied, "I am already doing this . . . isn't there something else for me to know?" The other people who were present thought his views to be too liberal, like those of 'Umar Khayyam (d. 1123, an Iranian mathematician and poet). For awhile Hazrat Hamid Hasan 'Alawi (r) listened to Hazrat and then said, "Follow the practices and see the results."

The few words of Hazrat Hamid Hasan 'Alawi (r) left a deep impact on Hazrat and he began his spiritual journey with great determination. Hazrat Hamid Hasan 'Alawi (r) returned home after a few days and instructed Hazrat to stay in touch with Hakim Ahsan Miyan, who was one of his disciples. Hazrat lived about five kilometers away from Hakim Ahsan's house. Hazrat's commitment was so strong that he walked to Hakim Sahib's house after supererogatory pre-dawn prayers (*tahajjud*) and performed the daily practices in the mosque with him. Hazrat's training up to the ten subtle centers of consciousness, was supervised by Hakim Ahsan Miyan as Hazrat Hamid Hasan 'Alawi (r) had instructed. During this time Hazrat had felt such an attachment and connection to Hakim Ahsan Miyan that he considered becoming initiated. However, even after completing his training in the ten subtle centers of consciousness Hazrat said that he was not fully convinced. Finally, after nine months he was fortunate enough to be able to be initiated by Hazrat Hamid Hasan 'Alawi (r).

With each passing day Hazrat became more immersed in his practices and the influence of Hakim Ahsan's spiritual company made him regular in the work and steadfast in his conviction. The Truth began to manifest itself more and more clearly in both the inner and outer aspects of his life. Also around this time in Allahabad, Hazrat found himself in the company of a person with inner spiritual experience called Mitthan Shah who liked him very much and often bestowed spiritual attention upon him. This helped to facilitate Hazrat's progress and higher levels of spirituality became accessible with great speed. Hazrat used to say that Mitthan Shah had a very high spiritual status and that he had achieved an awareness of his self. Mitthan Shah used to say, "When I am in the presence of angels I don't feel hungry, I only eat when I rejoin you people." Mitthan Shah always brought milk or dessert for Hazrat. When he stirred the milk for a little while, it turned into a delicious dessert.

By 1938, partly due to the practices and partly due to the influence of Mitthan Shah, Hazrat lost interest in his job. He resigned and returned home from Allahabad. Mitthan Shah also went with him but later took offence at something and returned to Allahabad. At this point, Hazrat's training had reached the second circle of the heart subtle center, and the practices occupied almost all of his time.[4] He did not care for food or drink, or anything else and spent night and day in the mosque absorbed in divine meditation.

Such were Hazrat's circumstances at home that at one time he had hardly any money left and the local shopkeeper refused to give him anymore groceries because he felt that Hazrat could not repay the loan. After eight months of being in this situation, Hazrat went to meet Hazrat Hamid Hasan 'Alawi (r). He told Hazrat that although the second circle had been completed (within eight months), a lot of hard work was still required. Yet he gave him the transmission for the third circle. Hazrat went back home in a completely altered state of mind. He told his mother that he had been given a new lease on life and there was no need to worry about anything anymore. After returning home from Allahabad, Hazrat continued his practices day and night for three years. This incessant struggle helped Hazrat make rapid progress. Hazrat had been with Hazrat Hamid Hasan 'Alawi (r) for only two years when he was granted permission to teach.

He had just started his training in the Chishti practices when Hazrat had a spiritual encounter with Hazrat Khwaja Mu'inuddin Chishti (r) (d. 1236 in Ajmer, India, and the founder figure of the Chishtiyya order in India). He was given a sign that he should go to Ajmer, but due to lack of resources he was unable to go right away. When he did eventually go, Hazrat Khwaja Mu'inuddin Chishti (r) communicated directly with him and expressed surprise at Hazrat's rapid progress. When Hazrat gave Hazrat Sayyid 'Abdul Bari Shah's (r) name as a reference, Hazrat Khwaja Mu'inuddin Chishti (r) did

4. The 'circles' are stations of spiritual attainment on the Sufi path. Please see page 65 for more detail on these stations.

not ask for further clarification and bestowed innumerable blessings on Hazrat during his stay in Ajmer. When Hazrat Hamid Hasan 'Alawi (r) heard about this incident he said, "Why didn't you write to me? If I had known I would have sent you the money to go to Ajmer, even if I had to sell my crop of rice to do it!"

Hazrat Hamid Hasan 'Alawi (r) then sent Hazrat to Calcutta to spread the teaching there. This is what Hazrat wrote about his trip. "It was in 1940 that I was first sent to Calcutta to spread the work of the order. The sight of the crowds in Howrah station caused me great distress. I was staying at the shrine of Hazrat Maula 'Ali (r) where there used to be large numbers of people out of control in their attraction to God (sing. *majdhub*). After eight days I was forced to leave in a state of bewilderment. I got off at Shah Ganj Station and immediately went to pay my respects to Hazrat [Hamid Hasan 'Alawi (r)]."

He had sent me off with many hopes and expectations, and was very surprised to see me return so soon without having accomplished anything. He asked, "What is the matter? Was there a problem with the eating and living arrangements?" I replied "No." He then asked, "Then why have you returned?" I said to him, "How will I fulfill my responsibility and who will listen to me in such a huge and over-populated city? I came back because I found my mission was too difficult." Hazrat (Hamid Hasan 'Alawi [r]) replied, "Go and spend time in remembrance of Allah. People who are destined to receive the teachings will come to you of their own accord." This statement provided such solace to Hazrat that he was not assailed by doubts any more. After the *chasht* prayer (a supererogatory prayer after sunrise) he gave such a profound recitation and transmission of the Holy Qur'an that the blessings of the Holy Qur'an became visible in a brilliantly luminous display, which lasted for quite awhile. Thus, all his self-doubts and hesitations were swept away. This statement of Hazrat Hamid Hasan 'Alawi's (r) became sanctified forever and henceforth became a beacon of guidance for seekers, its effect manifesting in amazing ways.

Mr. Mujib ur-Rahman of Tata Nagar had an intuition, which led him to come to Kohanda to seek a meeting with Hazrat Hamid Hasan 'Alawi (r). He requested Hazrat Hamid Hasan 'Alawi (r) to send somebody to spread the teachings in Tata Nagar, because there was a great need there. Hazrat Hamid Hasan 'Alawi (r) then suggested that Hazrat Maulvi Muhammad Sa'id Khan Sahib (r) should go to Tata Nagar to do the work of the order. He did so, and on arriving in this new place faced many internal and external obstacles. However, he remained undaunted and after several years of hard work the strength of evil forces dwindled and the way was paved for the work of the order. Whereas in the beginning there had been only Mr. Mujib ur-Rahman, very soon hundreds of people had joined the order.

Among Hazrat Sayyid 'Abdul Bari Shah's (r) deputies, Hazrat Hamid Hasan 'Alawi (r) had been given the responsibility for eastern India and Mr. 'Abdussamad had been given charge of western India. However, Mr. 'Abdussamad passed away soon after and therefore the work of the order in the west did not proceed as planned. There is no doubt that Hazrat Hamid Hasan 'Alawi (r) fulfilled the duties entrusted to him by Hazrat Sayyid 'Abdul Bari Shah (r) with the utmost zeal and commitment and his efforts led to many people joining the order in Purnia, Dhaka, Chittagong in Bangladesh, and in Burma. Due to his failing health however, Hazrat Hamid Hasan 'Alawi (r) was unable to visit these areas in the last few years of his life.

The deputies had started incorporating their own interpretation of the teachings, and this had caused divergence and a lack of uniformity in the practices. Hazrat Hamid Hasan 'Alawi (r) entrusted Hazrat Maulvi Muhammad Sa'id Khan (r) with the job of touring these areas, restoring uniformity to the teachings and re-organizing the work. Thus he began his teaching tours, and in a short while he had formed his own group. The other deputies co-operated with him and the work acquired uniformity. Under the supervision of Hazrat, the centers in these areas flourished and the work continued to be done on a large scale and with vigor. In this way, the order was re-organized in Bangladesh and Purnia and the work continued to progress.

Since I had found guidance after considerable search and investigation, I very much wanted to guide seekers of Truth so they could be saved from wandering off in the wrong direction. With the permission and blessings of Hazrat Hamid Hasan 'Alawi (r) and Hazrat, I also started teaching. Students from various provinces of India attended the Jamia, and my relationship with their guardians made my task a little easier. I started the work of the order in Hyderabad, Madras (now Chennai), Bangalore, Ahmadabad, and Jaipur among other places and undertook a six-week tour of these areas during the summer vacations.

I asked Hazrat to accompany me on my tours, and Hazrat graciously agreed. He had visited Delhi in 1940 with Hazrat Hamid Hasan 'Alawi's (r) deputy, Sufi 'Abdurra'uf (r), and had paid his respects at most of the shrines of the saints. In 1955 during the summer vacation, Hazrat arrived in New Delhi. From there we traveled to Madras (Chennai), Bangalore, Hyderabad, Bombay (Mumbai), Jaipur, and Ajmer. It became customary for us to go on this tour every year. Hazrat first came to Delhi, and then we spent around a month and a half touring. Afterwards Hazrat returned to Delhi, and then would go back home to Azamgarh. I went to Bandel a few times and Hazrat came there also. We then went on to tour Madras and other areas. In this way, every year, we did an all-India tour. Hazrat took great interest in these tours and as a result I was motivated, and many people joined the order in western and southern India.

*

In short, Hazrat's entire life was spent in struggle and tireless effort. He was involved in spreading the teaching and guiding disciples until the last days of his life. He was always busy teaching, sometimes in Bangladesh and Madras, other times in Malegaon and Bombay, and at other times in Karachi, Sind, and Lahore. He was unconcerned about his physical comfort and his health. Occasionally it happened that Hazrat felt weak and ill, but if someone happened to come to learn something from him he immediately called him in and would spend a long time in discussion. Hazrat used to say that he did not want to be held accountable for negligence and apathy. He often remarked that he had not been able to fulfill all the duties and obligations given to him by Hazrat Hamid Hasan 'Alawi (r), and he worried about having to answer for it on the Day of Judgment.

In the past mystics used to renounce the world and go into seclusion. They spent all their time practicing severe austerities to attain the goal, and this in itself was a great achievement. However, in my humble opinion, it is no less of an accomplishment to live in the world like any other member of society, to work and fulfill the responsibilities of life while not forgetting Allah for a single moment.

Hazrat spent the last part of his life living in the rented house behind the Jami' Masjid. Towards the end of his life, he had begun to suffer from indigestion and sore knees and could not go to the mosque to offer prayers. So he prayed at home. He seemed to be in an altered state and in a different sphere. It was as if he were preparing for a different kind of journey. Hazrat had become aware that the time had come for him to leave this transitory world. Although he often made references in this regard, his disciples were not able to grasp his meaning. When I went to visit Hazrat about six months before he passed away, I found him to be very weak and frail.

His followers wished Hazrat to recite the entire Holy Qur'an so they could record it. Sixteen parts had been completed. The person who was responsible for recording came at the appointed time, but Hazrat could only recite for a short time. He said that it was too strenuous for him to continue. Unable to bear the strain, he left the recording incomplete. Hazrat had lost his appetite, and it seemed that he was forcing himself to eat a few mouthfuls just to keep me company. When I took my leave of him he said, "May Allah grant us another meeting." This was not his usual form of leave-taking, but I failed to understand the full meaning of his statement. He had meant to let me know that there might not be another meeting. When his son 'Azduddin Miyan came to say goodbye, Hazrat turned his face away. 'Azduddin Miyan thought that perhaps his father was upset with him, but in reality, Hazrat had become aware that he would not see his son again and had turned his face away in order to conceal the depth of his emotions.

A colleague asked Hazrat why he had not been on any trips in the last few months. Hazrat replied, "This time I am planning a longer-than-usual trip." The person did not understand that Hazrat was telling him that he had received the "final invitation" and that he would be among us for only a few more days. The time had come for the soul to leave its temporary abode and to reunite with the Creator. However, there were no outward indications of this impending event. One day before his death, Hazrat received new followers whom he initiated. He instructed them, was involved in discussion until evening prayer, and was fine when he woke up the next morning. After completing his daily rituals, he reclined for a while and then remarked, "Death is a gift from God, an opportunity to meet one's Creator," and continued to talk to his grandson Asrar Miyan. On the 30th January 1976 at around ten o'clock in the morning his condition started to deteriorate rapidly, and by the time of the call to Friday noon prayer he had passed away.

Asrar Miyan, who was with him at the time, went into shock for a while but then recovered and informed the other relatives. Telegraphs were sent off to various places. Hazrat's son in Aligarh was informed and he arrived in Azamgarh to lead the funeral prayers. He said, "My father was very keen that I should have a telephone installed in my house and he was very happy when I finally did. Little did I know that he wanted the phone to be installed so that I could be informed of his death in time for the funeral." Hazrat's friends and relatives were devastated. As the news broke it seemed that all of Azamgarh arrived to mourn him. There was not a single person who was not in tears. Thus, leaving his followers and admirers mourning and lamenting, Hazrat set forth on a journey on which there is no looking back. Hazrat's son, 'Azduddin Miyan exhibited great fortitude and courage on this occasion, because this was not a misfortune that could be easily endured. He was numb with shock and his limbs felt lifeless, yet he pushed aside his grief and set about making the funeral arrangements. Seeing him so involved helped other people to recover from their grief. The body was taken from Azamgarh to Mangarawan and the burial took place at midnight.

I had visited Hazrat just before his death and had gone to Mangarawan with him from Azamgarh. One morning after breakfast, Hazrat suggested that we go to the farm. He then crossed the road and sat down on the exact spot where his shrine now stands. There were a few other people with us. Hazrat appeared to be in an inexplicable state as he spoke about the impermanence of the world. We sat there for a long time before returning home. At that time none of us understood the significance of this event, but later we realized that Hazrat had knowledge of the location of his last resting place.

*

Hazrat was a man of simple habits. He was usually dressed in a *kurta*, pajama, or *lungi* and wore a small cap. When he went to teach in school, he wore a formal tunic or jacket (*sherwani*) with a matching cap. No one could tell from looking at his dress that Hazrat was such a venerable and holy man. People generally knew him as Maulvi Sahib and that is why I have not addressed him as Shaykh al-Tariqat, Qutb al-Aqtab, Ghaus-i Zaman and the like, but have simply added the title Maulvi before his name. Occasionally, when we were together, people looked at my attire and mistakenly come towards me instead. Hazrat's meals were not lavishly prepared. If breakfast were not ready in time, he had the previous night's leftovers and left in order to arrive at school on time. When Mr. Abu'l-Hasan, with whom Hazrat was on friendly terms, was the principal of the school, he took special care to always be punctual and to reach school a few minutes ahead of time in order to avoid any misperceptions.

Hazrat avoided talking about his spiritually elevated state. He never tried to distinguish himself from others or seek any privileges for himself. Once Mr. Muzaffar Hussain, a disciple who also happened to be a Minister in Uttar Pradesh, was invited to visit Hazrat's school. Hazrat kept him company for a while, but soon joined the other teachers. Whenever we traveled by train, I used to insist that Hazrat should take the upper berth, but he told me to make his bed on the lower berth. In Ahmadabad there was a disciple named Sufi Siddiq who was too weak to climb up to the rooftop where Hazrat stayed, so Hazrat went down especially to meet and instruct him.

It is difficult to find a parallel for the discipline and organization that governed Hazrat's life. Although Hazrat worked at the school, fulfilled his responsibilities at home, and had other important duties and obligations, he did not allow any of this to distract him from his religious activities. On the occasion of the wedding of a son or daughter, Hazrat bore the burden of many extra responsibilities, but he never let his disciples sense any difference in his attention. He would meet with them as usual, hold discussions, and participate enthusiastically in the meditation and daily practices. As soon as the wedding celebrations were complete he set off on a tour to spread the order. Hazrat Hamid Hasan 'Alawi (r) would say, "Maulvi Sahib, you receive a lot of guests, you should buy a plot of land and build a house on it." Hazrat listened but did not reply, for he never focused on property or other material things lest these worldly objects became a distraction for him and hinder his religious work.

Hazrat was a very gracious man, and met newcomers with a smiling, cheerful countenance, making every attempt to remove their trepidation and put them at ease. Hazrat's colleague, Jamil Miyan, was the opposite in this respect. When a new seeker came to him he asked them if they could spare four hours a day for the practices. If the person responded in the negative, he sent them away. On the contrary, if a seeker told Hazrat that they could not devote much time to, nor be able to do all the daily practices, Hazrat told them to do as much as they were able to in the hope that in time things would be all right. If he met a seeker after a gap of a year and learned that the seeker had not put too much effort into the practices, he nevertheless gave them the next transmission in the hope that as the seeker progressed, even those transmissions that had not been developed would be affected.

Hazrat liked to designate one person in every region for the work of the order and encouraged all his disciples to be employed in some profession or other, so that the work of the order could proceed without being hampered by financial dependence. When Sufi

'Abdurra'uf passed away, the disciples in Malegaon pleaded with Hazrat to come to Malegaon and guide the disciples there. I accompanied Hazrat to Malegaon, and while Hazrat was giving transmissions he realized that Sufi 'Abdurra'uf (r) had already appointed a deputy, 'Abdullah Miyan, who used to make regular visits to the town. Hazrat admonished the people who had invited him to Malegaon, and immediately returned home.

If anyone asked for protective amulets he said, "Follow the example of Hazrat Sayyid 'Abdul Bari Shah (r), so that one glance from you is all that is required and there is no need for amulets." Hazrat also imparted guidance to jinns.[5] One night in Ahmadabad, the discourse continued late into the night. Many times Hazrat said "That is enough, give others a chance." Those who were present failed to understand that Hazrat was saying that other creatures such as jinns were waiting to receive guidance, and that they came to meet him wherever he traveled.

Hazrat's spiritual attention was very effective and powerful. One day he said, "I have to be careful in directing my attention lest the receiver be unable to endure it and his soul leaves his body." A yogi had heard that if one spent time with Muslim Sufis one's heart would awaken and become open. For years he had been searching for a Sufi who could help him attain this state. Eventually his search led him to Hazrat and he came to see him. It was evening, and as usual Hazrat was seated in a corner of the Jami' Masjid with his disciples. After a short conversation, Hazrat began giving the yogi spiritual transmission. After awhile the yogi felt his heart awaken, and he started dancing with joy. He left Hazrat saying, "I'm leaving now, but we'll meet again!"

Hazrat was a highly sensitive man. If a sick person came and sat next to him, he was cured of his affliction. There was once a gentleman who was suffering from a fatal disease who was acquainted with Hazrat and knew that his empathy and proximity acted as a cure for any disease. Hence, one morning he came and sat in the mosque and when Hazrat finished his daily practices this gentleman extended his hand for a handshake. Hazrat responded by extending his own hand. As soon as their hands met, the gentleman recovered from his illness, but Hazrat was so badly affected that he thought that he was about to pass away. He did recover after some time, but was in pain for a few days.

---

5. Jinn are beings who are created out of fire, are normally invisible to people, and either have religious affiliation or are malevolent.

Hazrat was not only an English-speaking scholar, but someone whom Allah had graced with His direct knowledge. When disciples or newcomers asked him questions, Hazrat's responses appeared to be based on divine inspiration rather than scholarly knowledge. Occasionally the divine inspiration was interrupted and then the reply was terse and unsatisfactory. Later, when he had received the complete inspiration, and the answer had become clear, he summoned me and provided a full explanation. Hazrat had extraordinary powers of dialogue and a genius for providing convincing responses to the questions he was asked. In Shibli Manzil he met the late Sayyid Sulaiman Nadavi who was not a believer in Sufism. For many days a discussion went on between them. On one occasion in Delhi, while Hazrat was my guest, people of divergent views happened to gather at my house. Each person asked questions in accordance with his own beliefs and soon a debate began. It was amazing to see Hazrat offer such compelling rebuttals to all the arguments. His answers were so logical that his opponent was left speechless. Once we were talking about metaphysical questions, Hazrat offered arguments that appeared to have been drawn from the book *Ramuz-i hikmat* (*The Signs of Wisdom*) by 'Allama Hakim Muhammad Sharif. However when I asked Hazrat about this, he said that he had never even seen the book!

Hazrat always practiced restraint and remained patient. He never let his disciples realize that he was aware of their inner states. People saw him reclining and assume that he was not paying attention to them, but he was aware of everything around him. One day he said to them, "I can tell you how many mouthfuls each of you has eaten." Once in awhile, when a disciple was inattentive and distracted, Hazrat noticed but refrained from admonishing them. When his disciples faltered in their practices, he often ignored it in the hope that they would change their attitude in time. During his last days however, when he was quite frail, he sometimes was less patient and was unable to refrain from admonishing heedless disciples, sending them away. One day he said, "People say Maulvi Sahib is very dry and harsh, little do they know how gentle I am on the inside. Like a coconut, I am tough outside but soft inside."

Hazrat had three sons and two daughters. Among his sons, Sa'duddin Miyan and Zafaruddin Miyan have passed away. 'Azduddin Miyan was a professor of Islamic Studies in Aligarh Muslim University. Hazrat's eldest son, Sa'duddin Miyan, died an untimely death in a train accident. When they heard the news, Hazrat and his family were devastated. 'Azduddin read of the accident in the newspaper at Aligarh and immediately went to Azamgarh. The body had been kept at the police station, and when Hazrat arrived, he took one look at the body and then went and sat down in the room. A close companion, Maulvi 'Aziz ur-Rahman remarked, "Maulvi Sahib, you are very hard-hearted! You haven't shed a single tear at the sight of your son's body!" Hazrat merely said, "Maulvi Sahib, the death of even a pet baby bird is cause for sorrow . . . this was my son, a piece of my heart." To his chosen disciples and close friends Hazrat explained that when he saw the body of his son, an ocean of tears seemed to well up within him but before he could shed any tears, a calm had descended upon him.

Hazrat's daughters were called Bibi Rizwana and Bibi 'Irfana. He was especially close to Bibi Rizwana with whom he had a special bond. She was the mother of Asrar Miyan, and under Hazrat's vigilant and enthusiastic supervision Bibi Rizwana committed the Holy Qur'an to memory. After she was married, she often came back to stay with Hazrat to make sure he was comfortable and well looked after. However, as God would have it, she was suddenly diagnosed with cancer. Prayers were made for her recovery and no effort was spared to provide her with the best possible medical treatment. However, her time had come and she passed away soon after.

Fortunately, in keeping with her wishes, Asrar Miyan was married during her lifetime and the event provided her with joy during her illness. Hazrat was deeply affected by this calamity but he did not make his feelings known to others. It was to be a long time before a smile crossed his face. When I went to Azamgarh after the tragedy, I took with me an engraved headstone for her tomb. Hazrat saw me coming at a distance and told me to put down the headstone. He was silent for awhile, then he said, "Just a couple of days ago, I saw Rizwana walking around in the house, as was her custom, and I asked her how she was and why she had come. She replied, "I have been given a special kind of life and that is why I have returned. Somebody has to take care of you."

Hazrat was constantly making plans to spread the teachings. His wish was to guide all people who were in search of the Truth, irrespective of their caste or creed. When he was at home he willingly taught all who came seeking the teaching. During the winter and summer holidays he went to different areas to promote the work of the order. In those days one could not reserve seats on the train. Sometimes the compartment got so crowded that he would have to sit in the same position for hours, unable to make the slightest movement. His feet swelled up, but his enthusiasm remained unabated. Later, when it became possible to make reservations in trains, Hazrat spent the time lying down. He appeared to be sleeping, but he was actually awake, conducting spiritual meetings and imparting knowledge to invisible beings inhabiting the various regions through which the train passed. Periodically, he would get up, have something to eat, say his prayers, and then lie down again and continue his spiritual work. Hazrat's daily routine remained unaffected whether he traveled or stayed at home.

I had heard it said that, "Sufis live *in* the world but are not *of* the world." I had read in praise of the Naqshbandi path that "hands may be involved in ordinary work, but the heart is always attentive to the Beloved." Hazrat exemplified these principles; he was constantly engaged in remembrance of God and he seemed unaffected by the cares of the world. Outwardly, he appeared to be attending to any essential concerns that might have arisen, but inwardly he did not falter for even one single moment in his remembrance of God.

Hazrat spent the greater part of his life in a small, run-down house. He was more concerned about the residents than the residence. Numerous friends, and even people who did not agree with him, came to see him in that house and had their desires fulfilled, becoming disciples and singing Hazrat's praises. His powers were such that he could help a seeker reach an elevated spiritual status that normally took many years in a matter of days. Even disciples who lived in faraway places benefited from Hazrat's attention and were able to reach advanced levels. In short, although Hazrat resided in Azamgarh, the radiance of his being not only illuminated India from one end to the other, but reached foreign countries as well.

Whenever I used to be in Hazrat's holy presence, I sensed that he was very busy and preoccupied and didn't have a moment to spare. Upon my arrival he asked about my health and welfare, and then become absorbed in his spiritual work. Out of respect I dared not speak, and yet blessings continued to be bestowed on me. His benevolence and affection was manifested in numerous other forms. His kindness was such that he always sent me off with chilli pickle and potato and meatball curry. Hazrat possessed all the qualities of a perfect human being (*insan-i kamil*). Such individuals are not just rare, but impossible to find. It is my prayer that people will read about his life and be inspired. I hope that they will follow his teachings and devise a solid and comprehensive plan to combat anti-religious ideologies.

*

At this point in the narrative, the reader might wonder why I have not made any mention of Hazrat's visions and miracles. I would like to tell a story about Hazrat Khwaja Mu'inuddin Chishti (r). Once Hazrat Khwaja Mu'inuddin Chishti (r) put his hand on a murder victim and said, "O victim, if you were killed through no fault of your own, then may God command you to rise up!" These words had barely passed his exalted lips when the murdered person came to life. On that occasion, Hazrat Khwaja Mu'inuddin Chishti (r) said, "One should develop such a deep affinity with Allah that whatever one asks for is granted. He who has not been able to develop his relationship to this extent is not worthy of being called a friend of Allah (*wali*)." Others may or may not measure up to this standard, but Hazrat fulfilled this criterion in every respect. The visions Hazrat had in a conscious state are usually only perceived and experienced in a state of drifting and spiritual ecstasy by others. One day, while he was experiencing such a state of spiritual ecstasy Hazrat said, "If I told clay to speak it would." Events that were nothing short of miracles occurred routinely, but Hazrat attached little importance to them, and also discouraged his disciples from doing so. They treated the miracles as everyday occurrences.

While teaching at the Shibli School, it so happened that the Arabic curriculum and prescribed text were changed halfway through the year. Hazrat was not made aware of the changes and continued using the old textbook. When he received notification of the changes to the curriculum a short while before the final examination, the students and the Principal were very alarmed and dismayed. Hazrat told his students to stay calm and not to worry. A couple of days before the exam, he gave the students a list of questions to prepare. On the day of the exam, the students were delighted to see that the very same questions had appeared on their examination paper. Thus Hazrat's students passed the examination easily.

On one occasion, during the course of a conversation, Hazrat said to his son-in-law Iftikhar Miyan, "Only the people I *want* to meet come to my house. If I don't want to see someone, they are not able to visit me." Upon hearing this Iftikhar Miyan challenged him, "You will see, I will come here even if you don't want me to!" For three months after the challenge Iftikhar Miyan tried his level best to see Hazrat but was unable to do so until Hazrat finally decided that he wanted to see Iftikhar Miyan. It was then that, full of remorse, Iftikhar Miyan arrived in Hazrat's presence.

When I went to see Hazrat to offer my condolences for the death of his eldest son Sa'duddin Miyan, Hazrat told me that he had had prior knowledge of this event. The deceased had asked his mother to persuade his father to give him some money for a new business venture and the family had talked for a long time. Hazrat said that prior knowledge of his son's impending demise was not enough to avert the will of Allah. The following morning, he had breakfast and took his leave of Hazrat who had given him some money. Three hours later Hazrat received news of the accident.

On one occasion, the late Mr. Muhammad 'Ali came from Jaipur to visit Hazrat in Azamgarh. He had barely shaken hands with Hazrat and sat down when Hazrat said, "You can have tea at the station." Mr. Muhammad 'Ali was stunned, but wanted to comply with Hazrat's wishes so he promptly left for Jaipur. It transpired that his presence had been necessary to complete a business transaction and he would have incurred a substantial loss had he not returned when he did. On yet another occasion, Hazrat went to Bihar for the work of the order. He arrived at his disciple's home according to plan, but found that the members of the household appeared unusually dejected and in low spirits. Upon being asked, the head of the household gestured towards a room and explained that the room had become locked by itself and no matter how hard they tried, they had been unable to unlock it. Upon hearing this, Hazrat got up to investigate. When he approached the door, it opened of its own accord and Hazrat went in and said, "We will stay in this room." The faces of the family members lit up with joy, because all the meditation and daily practices were conducted in the room. Initially some beings could be heard walking on the roof but after a few days, tranquility ensued.

While I was working as a principal, Mr. Asrar, a native of Azamgarh, worked as a common office boy in the school. I was very keen that Mr. Asrar should be initiated by Hazrat, but sensed some reluctance on Mr. Asrar's part. It occurred to me that his subordinate position in the school was preventing him from becoming initiated. One day I happened to meet Mr. Asrar in Hazrat's house in Azamgarh and I seized the opportunity to suggest that Hazrat accept Mr. Asrar as his disciple. Hazrat asked Mr. Asrar a few questions regarding his pir (spiritual guide), but he did not show any inclination to become initiated. Later Hazrat told me that Mr. Asrar's pir had appeared to him and requested that Mr. Asrar be allowed to stay on the path he was on.

On one occasion, I accompanied Hazrat on a trip from Tata Nagar to Orissa. Hazrat was traveling in first class while I was in the second-class compartment. My compartment happened to be insufferably crowded and my shawl was lost in the crowd. In my distress I decided to get my ticket changed to first class, but Hazrat told me not to do so. Nevertheless, I found the congested compartment unbearably suffocating and so I had my ticket changed, and went and sat with Hazrat in the first-class compartment. After we had passed through a couple of stations, Hazrat left the compartment and suggested that we should try to locate my shawl. To my astonishment, the same compartment that had been so overcrowded was almost vacant and the remaining passengers were stretched out on the berths! Hazrat looked at me and smiled. The implication was that if I had listened to him and exhibited some patience and forbearance, I would have ended up being more comfortable in the second-class compartment.

Instances like these abounded in Hazrat's life. Hazrat used to wake up just before someone arrived for an unannounced visit. Whenever Hazrat desired to see someone that person was somehow drawn to visit him. Once a follower wrote regarding a difficult pregnancy caused by the baby being in an awkward position in the womb. Hazrat held the letter in his hand for a while before setting it aside. The next day news arrived that the baby's position had suddenly changed and that the delivery had taken place with great ease! Such was the result of a few moments of Hazrat's attention. On some occasions, Hazrat's presence used to fill the mosque with luminosity and the blessings were clearly visible in a waking state and even witnessed by strangers. In Bhopal, the way to where Hazrat was staying was through a graveyard. While passing through one day, Hazrat stopped for a short time. I happened to be accompanying him that day and asked him the reason for pausing there. Hazrat replied, "The deceased had been asking for intercession on their behalf, therefore I turned my attention towards them, and Allah showed his mercy."

Hazrat used to say "The general public measures the greatness of mystics by their ability to perform miracles that lead to the attainment of worldly objectives. However, those days are past when miracles provided testament to the Divine Truth and people were accepting Islam in droves. These days, Hindu yogis and *sadhus* are also able to perform miracles. How are we going to differentiate between them and ourselves? This is why Hazrat Sayyid 'Abdul Bari Shah (r) said, "that to bring life to a dead man is not as great a miracle as awakening and enlightening a heart."

Hazrat did not give much importance to the art of predicting the future. In his opinion, the ability to perform miracles was just a bonus and he did not consider it to be an indispensable requisite for the achievement of spiritual excellence. He attached more importance to following the sunna than to any other spiritual exercises and endeavors. He was of the opinion that the blessings and illuminations that resulted from following the sunna were superior to any other. He considered inner tranquility and the co-presence of God better than the state of divine inebriation. He used to say that everyone knows that the Companions (R) of the Prophet (S) did not manifest these types of miracles.[6] As the practices of our order are in accordance with the Holy Qur'an, the sunna, and the practices of the Companions (R) and their followers (r), it follows therefore that the disposition of the shaykhs of our order is like that of the Companions (R).

On one occasion in particular, Hazrat spoke emphatically and with great intensity on this topic. He said, "You should not rejoice if a miracle manifests itself to you. Remember that the great Sufis went to extraordinary lengths to conceal the miracles they experienced. The devout and learned person eschews miracles lest they start to be relished. Allowing the love of miracles to take root in your heart is akin to taking poison. Don't limit your ambition and endeavors to the desire to walk on water and soar in the air because even birds and fish are capable of such feats. Aspire to soar towards the Infinite Presence because to bypass the Benefactor and become enraptured by His beneficence is a sign of weak resolve and the absence of inner knowledge."

---

6. *Radiya Allahu 'anhu/'anha'* abbreviated as (R) means 'May God be pleased with him/her' and is used after the names of the Companions (R).

Chapter Two

The End is Included in the Beginning: The Revival of the Teaching of Sufism

The goal of Sufism is the development of certain noble qualities such as the purification of the self, purification of the heart, moral etiquette, doing what is beautiful (*ihsan*), nearness to God, inner knowledge (*ma'rifat*), annihilation in God (*fana'*), and subsistence in God (*baqa'*). In short, the true purpose of Sufism is to transform the seeker into a highly humane and moral person by building the seeker's character through spiritual training.

In different places in the Holy Qur'an there are verses that clearly address the effort to acquire these noble qualities and point to the highest stations of nearness to and realization of God. The qualities or attributes that Sufism seeks to develop have been alluded to in the following examples taken from the Holy Qur'an and the hadith:

Allah bestowed favor on the believers when He sent them a messenger from among themselves, to recite to them Allah's signs to purify them and to teach them Scripture and wisdom. Before they had been in manifest error. (Qur'an 3:164) According to this verse of the Holy Qur'an there are four important duties of the messenger and the purification of people's inner selves is one of the most important. Sufis place great emphasis on the purification of the self because until a person becomes purified, it is impossible to follow Islamic law (*shari'a*) sincerely. The Sufis have made a priority of purification, passing their whole lives in the fulfillment of this duty as deputies of the prophets (s).

*

A verse of the Qur'an (4:136) states, *O you who believe! Believe in Allah and His Messenger.* In this verse believers are being commanded to believe. Until the self has been cleansed, the self is rebellious and impure. It has not attained true annihilation, so the true purpose of divine law cannot be achieved. Only after annihilation can the treasure of contentment be obtained. Just as before achieving peace there is the external observance of the shari'a, after peace has been achieved inner knowledge (*ma'rifat*) is possible. The kind of faith that ordinary people possess is unaware because it has its ups and downs. It is weak and surrounded by dangers. True faith is the faith bestowed upon the elect, the people of the Truth, and is protected from doubt or vacillation. The more this faith is rooted in the annihilation of the self, the more perfect it is. The Holy Qur'an (49:14) alludes to this kind of faith. *The Bedouin say "We believe." Say [to them]: "You do not have faith. Instead say "We have submitted," since faith has not yet entered your hearts.* The meaning of this verse is that true belief has still not taken root in their hearts. The Sufis have devised different methods to help the seeker attain this state of unflinching faith more easily, thus allowing faith to enter the seeker's heart.

*

Another Qur'anic verse (73:8) says, *Remember the name of your Lord and devote yourself to Him wholeheartedly.* This means that the remembrance of God should fully occupy the heart night and day. The person should be occupied with remembering God every minute of the day, and that which is other than God should not distract him or her from God for even a moment. A person should separate him or herself from all relationships and only one relationship should remain in one's inner self. The Sufi's aim and object is to create this station in people. With the help of Sufi practices, seekers can more easily attain this attitude of remembrance.

*

One who purifies it succeeds. And one who corrupts it fails (Qur'an 91:9-10). The Sufis understand that the cleansing of the self requires its purification and refinement. One's passions have to be made subservient to the intellect, and the intellect needs to be ruled by divine law so that the spirit and the heart are both enlightened through divine illumination. When passions and appetites are allowed to govern the self it then becomes impure. The intellect and divine law become irrelevant and the person simply becomes an embodiment of desires. Such a human being lives a life that is worse than that of an animal.

*

In another verse of the Holy Qur'an (87:14-15) God reveals, *One who purifies it will succeed and pray remembering the name of the Lord.* Sufis purify themselves of external and inner impurities and perfect themselves through adorning themselves with right belief, excellent moral conduct, and righteous deeds. There is no doubt that such a person is successful.

*

A famous hadith narrated by Hazrat 'Umar (R) states, "One day when we were in the presence of the Prophet of God (S), a man suddenly appeared. No mark of travel was visible on him and none of us recognized him. He came and sat down in front of the Prophet (S) and said, "O Muhammad, tell me about submission to God (*islam*)." The Prophet (S) told him about submission to God. The man heard the reply and said, "You have spoken the truth." Then he asked about faith (*iman*). The Prophet (S) explained faith to him. On hearing the Prophet's (S) reply the man said, "You have spoken the truth." After this he then said, "Now tell me about doing what is beautiful (*ihsan*)." The Prophet (S) replied, "Doing what is beautiful means that you should worship God as if you see Him, for even if you do not see him, he sees you." On hearing the Prophet's (S) reply he once again said, "You have spoken the truth." One of the important goals of Sufism is to create the state of doing what is beautiful. Though different shaykhs have used different terms for doing what is beautiful in this context, they are trying to assist others to create the same state of doing what is beautiful like the Prophet Muhammad (S) used to do.

*

The Prophet (S) said that God said, "The best thing that you can do to obtain nearness to me is to fulfill the duties I have made obligatory. Nearness to me is achieved most of all through the fulfillment of duties."

Through voluntary acts the seeker keeps coming closer to me until such time as I begin to love him/her. When I begin to love him or her I become the ears with which the person hears, the eyes with which the person sees, the hands with which the person holds, and the feet with which the person walks. And if the person asks me for something I bestow it. And if the person seeks refuge from something I give that person refuge.[1]

---

1. This is one of the *hadith qudsi*, a non-Qur'anic transmission from God to Muhammad (S).

Hazrat Musa Ash'ari (R) narrates, "We were on a journey with the Prophet (S) and people were reciting the *takbir* very loudly."[2] The Prophet (S) said, "O people be kind to your selves. Lower your voice when you recite the *takbir*. You are not calling someone who is absent or who cannot hear. You are calling upon someone who hears and sees, someone who is with you and nearer to you than the neck of your camel." The Prophet (S) said, "Allah says that I deal with my servants in accordance with their opinion of me, and when my servants remember me, I'm with them, and if my servants remember me in their heart, then I too remember them in my heart, and if my servants remember me in a gathering I remember them in a better gathering, a gathering of angels. And if my servants direct their attention towards me, I direct my attention to them many times over. And if my servants walk towards me, I run towards them."

*

These verses and hadith clearly show how necessary nearness to Allah and knowledge of the Truth is for a believer. During the time of the Prophet (S) these noble characteristics were cultivated by obeying God's commandments as revealed in the Holy Qur'an and through the company of the Prophet (S), his attention, and power of spiritual influence. After the Prophet's (S) death, as time passed, these qualities became less and less common in people. To address this deterioration, and perfect the seeker's relationship with religion, i.e., to acquire divine secrets and inner attributes, the purification of the self, the quality of doing what is beautiful (*ihsan*) and nearness to God, different Sufi shaykhs devised ways of attaining inner knowledge on the basis of their own experience within the framework of the Islamic law. This was undertaken in a way that was similar to the way in which Islamic scholars codified and developed jurisprudence through logical deduction and sincere striving. These laws took many centuries to be codified after the lifetime of the Prophet (S).

There is no doubt spiritual perfection and spiritual stations all benefit from the blessings of the Prophet (S). All Sufi orders are associated with the Prophet (S) and trace their spiritual lineage back to him (S). Shaykhs and their lineages have all received their spiritual affinity (*nisbat*) from the Prophet (S). This spiritual affinity is derived from the light of the Prophet (S) and is recorded in hadiths.

2. The recitation of *Allahu akbar* (God is greatest).

However, for ease of understanding, it was the Sufis who classified this spiritual affinity into categories such as annihilation in God, subsistence in God, attraction to God (*jadhba*), the path of spiritual practices (*suluk*), and the journey towards God (*sayr ila Allah*).

As far as the goal of Sufism is concerned, there is little difference of opinion among the Sufis. However, there are some differences in methods of achieving the goal. These differences are natural because the methods are based on the spiritual experiences of individual Sufi shaykhs. The destination is the same for everyone, but the paths are different. Sufis say there are as many paths to Allah as there are souls of human beings.

On the basis of methodology, Sufis can be divided into two groups. The first group focuses on love as the most fundamental thing, for love is the secret of life. To annihilate one's self in God is considered to be one of the most exalted goals of the spiritual journey. In the Holy Qur'an (2:165) we read, *those of faith love Allah more ardently.* Without any doubt the result of belief in God is love of God. The Prophet's (S) life was one of immersion in the love of God. He used to pray, "O God, make my love for thee dearer to me than my life, my family, and cool water." When the love of God dwells in a human being's heart no thought or action remains unaffected by it and the seeker's entire life changes. The question is however, how can a human being develop such love for God?

There are hundreds of things that distract human beings from turning their attention towards God. The heart is at times entangled in wealth, desires, and at other times, with a beloved, family, or business. The involvement of one's heart in thousands of desires is a great obstacle in turning one's attention towards God. The shaykhs realized this. The remedy proposed was that the seeker should find a shaykh who has attained divine perfection, because the Prophet (S) has said about such people, "When you see them you remember God. They are near to God and in their company you find the reflection of those who are dear to God." On finding such an extraordinary person, the seeker should hand him or herself over, focus their heart on the shaykh, and annihilate themselves in the shaykh (*fana' fi'l shaykh*). This enables the heart to detach itself from everything and allow it to turn in one direction, developing its capacity to direct its attention to God. The remedy was not in and of itself the goal; it was a means for fulfilling the need of the people. Once the seeker's attention is focused on one point and the seeker can turn the attention towards God, the shaykh steps aside and turns the seeker's attention towards the love of the Prophet (S) so that the seeker may attain the station of annihilation in the Prophet (S) (*fana' fi'l-rasul*). After this, the third and last station is that of annihilation in God (*fana' fillah*), where the heart is directly connected to God. This is a station very few reach.

The second group's understanding is that the love of God depends on the complete purification of the self and its true spirit is humility. The most important figure from this group was Hazrat 'Abdul Khaliq Ghujduwani (r) (d. ca 1179). He formulated some basic principles that served as the foundation for the establishment of this group. Everyone knows that love is a great force that takes human beings to God, but only a person who has freed himself from the self is capable of this love. This task was very difficult to accomplish and few seekers can reach this station.

The shaykhs and teachers of this second group reject the teaching methods of the first group. The second group's methods for spiritual progress involve spiritual attraction, spiritual attention/transmission, keeping the company of the shaykh, and following the sunna. The most important feature of their method is 'spontaneous divine attraction'. *Allah chooses for Himself those whom He wants and guides to Himself those who repent.*[3] (Qur'an 42:13)

The first group of Sufis gives priority to the path of spiritual practices whereby the seeker undertakes a detailed outward journey through each of the ten stations.[4] In the second group, the seeker obtains a general overview of the ten stations as a whole because the blessings have absorbed him or her in love so that the seeker cannot get involved in the details of these stations. Instead, due to love, the essence of these stations is completely and fully received by the seeker.

The spiritual journey is a very long one and involves facing great trials and hardships. It could take a lifetime - the seeker often dying before reaching the final destination. This is why Hazrat Khwaja Baha'uddin Naqshband (r) (d. 1389 and the founder figure of

3. In letter 1.292 Shaykh Sirhindi (r) states that there are two kinds of wayfarers on this path: those desiring God (*murid*) and those desired by God (*murad*). Those desired by God are blessed by the path of love and attraction to God as they are strongly attracted and carried along, arriving at the highest goal.

4. The ten stations are: repentance, asceticism, total trust in God, contentment, solitude, continual remembrance, attention, patience, meditation, and satisfaction.

the Naqshbandiyya order), in accordance with the will of Allah, put attraction to God before the path of spiritual practices (*suluk*). Unlike in the first group of Sufis, spiritual training is given not through the subtle centers of consciousness of the world of creation (*'alam-i khalq*) comprising the self (*nafs*) and the four gross elements that make the physical frame (*anasir-i arb'a*),[5] but through the subtle centers of consciousness of the world of divine command (*'alam-i amr*): heart (*qalb*), spirit (*ruh*), secret (*sirr*), hidden (*khafi*) and most hidden (*akhfa*). Attention is given to these subtle centers of consciousness so that they can merge and be annihilated in their original forms in the higher, subtler realms. This is known as the journey within the inner self (*sayr-i anfusi*). It is after the purification of the heart that the hard work involved in the purification of the self and the four gross elements of the body is undertaken. In this way, through practice and the attention of the shaykh, these subtle centers are purified.

This method of spiritual travel is known as 'the end is included in the beginning' (*indiraj al-nihayat fi'l-bidayat*). This is because the attraction to God that the seekers of the first group find at the end of their spiritual journey is already present at the beginning of the journey for the second group. In this way, spiritual travel can be accomplished more easily and quickly. It should be clear that only a taste of the attraction to God and the love that is received by those who are near the end of their journey is given to the second group at the beginning. However, the full reality of attraction to God is revealed only at the end of the journey, even to the seekers of the second group who have devised a special method for attaining this. Thus there is a particular brilliance about their attraction to God.

In the teaching that Hazrat received from Hazrat Hafiz Hamid Hasan 'Alawi (r), which he in turn received from Hazrat Sayyid 'Abdul Bari Shah (r), spiritual training is given through spiritual

---

5. The universe is known as the *'alam-i kabir*. The upper half of the circle is known as *'alam-i amr* (the world of command) and the lower half is known as the *'alam-i khalq* (world of creation). Principles, realities, possibilities, and the souls of all living beings inhabit the world of command. The world of creation has to do with imperfections, duration, and time. It is also known as the world of physical forms. Individual souls and physical forms are determined by the world of command, which includes the heavens, hell, the throne (*'arsh*), angels, jinn, and the Preserved Tablet (*luh-i-mahfuz*). The earth, human beings, animals, plants, and all living and non-living things belong to the world of creation.

attention/transmission, spiritual affinity and the awakening of the subtle centers of consciousness. The teaching is given in accordance with the principle of 'the end is included in the beginning'. For this training, remembrance of God, recitation of the blessings on the Prophet (S) and his family, meditation, awareness of the heart, and spiritual friendship with the shaykh are obligatory. This approach is one of association with the shaykh because it is through spiritual association with the shaykh that seekers can truly realize their full potential and are transformed.

The following passages further explicate the key principles, terms, and teaching methods mentioned in the preceding paragraphs. They characterize the teaching practices of the five major Sufi paths. The development of the teaching methods, initiated by Hazrat Khwaja Baha'uddin Naqshband (r), furthered by Hazrat Shaykh Ahmad Faruqi Sirhindi (r), then developed even further as a spiritual curriculum for seekers by Hazrat Sayyid 'Abdul Bari Shah (r) and initiated in the West by Hazrat Maulvi Muhammad Sa'id Khan Sahib (r) are explained in detail here. This is to highlight the significant contribution of these shaykhs in reviving Sufism as a spiritual practice for the contemporary age.

In particular, the principle of 'the end is included in the beginning' and the key teaching techniques of spiritual attention/transmission, spiritual affinity, subtle centers of consciousness, remembrance of God, meditation, and awareness of the heart are explained. This prepares the reader for the following chapter, which discusses in detail the ways in which Hazrat Maulvi Muhammad Sa'id Khan Sahib (r) taught the practices and guided his students towards the knowledge and realization of God.

The End is Included in the Beginning (*indiraj al-nihayat fi'l-bidayat*)

Human beings forget their Creator for two reasons. The first is because human beings are drawn to the external world. The other reason involves the human being's egoic self, and what is to be found within it. To obtain nearness with God (*ma'iyyat*), it is necessary to free oneself from the slavery of both the external world and the sense of being a separate self (I-ness, which is ego). Most shaykhs first focus on freeing the seeker from the external world.

They give priority to the purification of the subtle centers of consciousness of the world of creation: the self, and the four gross elements (air, fire, water, and earth) that compose the physical human body. This journey is accomplished through rigorous spiritual practices and takes a very long time. If someone follows this path, and if something goes wrong in the long period that it takes to complete it, the seeker is not able to reach the goal.

Hazrat Khwaja Baha'uddin Naqshband (r) was aware of the significant risk seekers faced when undertaking this journey. He felt that as the distance from the period of prophethood increased, seekers' capacity and ability to traverse the spiritual path had deteriorated. Seekers no longer had the same dedication, passion, and courage. Keeping this in view, Hazrat Khwaja Baha'uddin Naqshband (r) with God's help, discovered a shorter and easier method, the inverse of the method being practiced at that time.

He focused first on the purification of the heart and then went through activating the four other subtle centers of consciousness of the world of divine command. Only then did he deal with the subtle centers of the world of creation. This is principally why this method is known as 'the end is included in the beginning'. With this method, as discussed previously, seekers are given just a taste of the final destination in the initial stages of the journey, with the seeker only fully understanding its reality at the end. Hazrat Khwaja Baha'uddin Naqshband (r) said that this method was quick and it involved neither great austerities nor great hardships, but allowed seekers a brief but sufficient survey of the path. In this way the details of the path are left for later and every effort is made to reach the final destination as quickly as possible.

Hazrat Shaykh Ahmad Faruqi Sirhindi (r) appeared like a sun on the firmament of guidance. He made this path of reaching the highest station one that is of greatest benefit to the most people. In taking this path to its zenith, he illuminated the world. He described the details of the world of divine command and systematized the teachings. Hazrat Shaykh Ahmad Faruqi Sirhindi (r) said that if seekers are engaged in detail with God's names and attributes, their path to God is obstructed because there is no end to the names and attributes of God. Practicing this method, only those seekers completing the journey in detail can reach the final destination.

In the light of a blessed hadith – that human beings should be treated with love, and that things should be made easy rather than difficult for them, Hazrat Sayyid 'Abdul Bari Shah (r) made a number of significant changes in Mujaddidi practices. Hazrat Sayyid 'Abdul Bari Shah (r) was the spiritual axis of his time and as a renewer of religion (*mujaddid*) was able to introduce the principle of 'the end is included in the beginning' to the rest of the orders with the consent of their founders. Shaykhs of some other orders also wanted to introduce this principle to their own teaching, but were not in a position to make changes. The qualities, spiritual status, and miracles of a renewer of religion, through God's help, facilitate the opening of new paths. There is no doubt that this was a historical feat of revival in the development of Sufi training and education.

Spiritual Transmission (*tawajjuh*)

Many scholars consider the angel Gabriel's (s) three embraces during the first revelation to the Prophet (S) a form of transmission. We can conclude that the knowledge that Gabriel (s) brought from God began with this transmission. The Prophet (S) was in the cave of Hira when Gabriel (s) came and asked him to recite. He said, "I cannot recite." Gabriel (s) embraced the Prophet (S), then pressed the Prophet (S) to him, declaring "Recite." The Prophet (S) replied, "I cannot." For the third time Gabriel (s) seized the Prophet (S) and said, "Recite." The Prophet (S) then recited the message of God (Qur'an 96:1-5): *Recite in the name of your Sustainer who created. He created the human being from an embryo. Recite! Your Lord is the most Generous. He taught by the Pen, teaching humans what they did not know.*

According to a hadith, one day the Prophet (S) was holding the hand of Hazrat 'Umar (R). 'Umar said to him, "O Allah's Apostle! You are dearer to me than everything except my own self." The Prophet (S) said, "No, by Him in whose hand my soul is, [you will not have complete faith] until I am dearer to you than your own self." Then Hazrat 'Umar (R) said to him, "However, now by Allah, you are dearer to me than my own self." The Prophet (S) said, "Now, O 'Umar, [now you are a believer]." This was without doubt the result of transmission.

The following incident was related by Hazrat Alja bin Ka'b (R). "When I was in the mosque, a man came in and started to say his prayers. He recited the Holy Qur'an in a manner that appeared incorrect to me. Then another man came in and recited the Holy Qur'an in yet another way. I went to the Prophet (S) and told him how these people had recited the Qur'an. The Prophet (S) asked both men to recite the Holy Qur'an and they did. The Prophet (S) then said that both were right. My heart was filled with evil doubt that was even stronger than that of the period of ignorance (*jahiliyya*). When the Prophet (S) saw my state, he struck my breast with his hand. I started perspiring profusely and my state of fear and awe was such that I felt I was seeing God.

In addition to these examples, there are many other incidents that can be cited as evidence of the effects of spiritual transmission. Once many Muslim scholars gathered together in Kohanda (Hazrat Hamid Hasan 'Alawi's (r) ancestral village) for a religious gathering. The conclusion they reached through their discussion was that transmission was not an effective method. They said if it had been effective, Abu Jahal and Abu Lahab would not have remained deprived of the blessings of guidance.[6] After the speeches, Hazrat Hamid Hasan 'Alawi (r) said, "Friends, this is not something that should be argued about. If someone is given spiritual transmission and is affected by it, then its efficacy should be believed in, otherwise not."

However, it is true that spiritual transmission and spiritual affinity are not the real source of the effect: God said (to Muhammad (S)), *You do not guide those whom you like, but Allah guides those whom He will* (Qur'an 28:56). The attainment of the final goal is not possible without God's grace. However, by following the sunna and the sayings, actions, company, and through the guidance and spiritual attention of saints and shaykhs, it is not impossible.

Spiritual Affinity (*nisbat*)

The word *nisbat* in Arabic means an affinity or connection between two people. In Sufi terminology, it is the affinity that develops between God and human beings. The essence of Sufism is that a person should develop some quality or virtue to such a degree, that it should permeate that person's being utterly. When such a quality becomes an essential part of one's being, it can be termed spiritual affinity. The objective of the Sufi quest is the attainment of this spiritual affinity.

There are many different types of affinity: the affinity of doing what is beautiful, the affinity of purity, the affinity of intense love, the affinity of spiritual ecstasy, the affinity of unity, the affinity of peace, and the affinity of remembrance, among others. It would, however, not be correct to assume that these affinities can only be obtained through Sufi practices. The exercises are only a means of achieving these. In reality, these are God's gift that He bestows on whomever He wills without consideration of spiritual lineage. In

6. These are the Prophet's (S) uncles who opposed him and became his arch enemies.

this regard, the statement of Hazrat Khwaja Baha'uddin Naqshband (r) is the most comprehensive. Someone asked him about the saints of his lineage, and he replied, "I did not reach God through the saints of my lineage. An attraction to God was bestowed upon me and that is what took me to God."

The Companions (R) and the followers of the Prophet (S) who came later, used to obtain spiritual affinity through different means. Consistency and regularity in the performance of the five obligatory daily prayers, voluntary prayers, constant praise of God, the recitation of the Holy Qur'an, the remembrance of death, and the fear of the Day of Judgment lead to the quality of nearness to God becoming ingrained in their hearts. For the rest of their lives they guard this affinity, for it is the same path that has come from the Prophet (S) to the shaykhs of different orders.

Subtle Centers of Consciousness (*lata'if*)

The names of some of the subtle centers of consciousness, such as the heart, self, and secret, were prevalent in the times of Hazrat Junayd al-Baghdadi (r) (d. 910) and his contemporaries. Later the list was expanded when the deputy of Hazrat Najmuddin Kubra (r) (d. 1049), Hazrat Najmuddin Razi (r) (d. 1256) added intellect (*'aql*) and hidden subtle centers. Hazrat 'Ala'udawla Simnani (r) (d. 1336) then added two more, and presented a sketch of a system based on seven subtle centers of consciousness where he described their colors and identified the prophets (s) with which each was associated. The deputy of Hazrat Khwaja Baha'uddin Naqshband (r), Hazrat Khwaja Muhammad Parsa (r) (d. 1420), spoke about the subtle centers of consciousness in a manner that was similar to Hazrat Simnani (r). Finally, Hazrat Shaykh Ahmad Faruqi Sirhindi (r), on the basis of his own investigation, identified ten subtle centers of consciousness in the human body. Not only did he give details of their location and color, but he also proceeded to devise an entire system for spiritual training based on the ten subtle centers of consciousness. He did this so that seekers could focus on the all-integrating subtlety in the human body and, with its help, travel the spiritual path with ease.

According to Hazrat Shaykh Ahmad Faruqi Sirhindi's (r) findings, parts of both the world of command and the world of creation are to be found within human beings. The ten subtle centers are in these two worlds. Five of these, namely heart, spirit, secret, hidden, and most hidden are related to the world of command. These constitute the inner aspects of human beings, while the other five pertain to the world of creation, i.e., the self and the four gross elements constituting the physical form of the human being. The location of these subtle centers of consciousness is the entire body, and their perfection means that the remembrance of God should emanate from every pore, "the supreme way to remember God." According to Hazrat Shah Wali'ullah (r) (d.1762), God created six subtle centers in human beings, each with their unique reality.

These subtle centers of consciousness are each associated with a particular color: yellow for the heart, red for the spirit, white for the secret, black for the hidden, and green for the most hidden. The self (*nafs*) subtle center is colorless. God has placed these unique faculties in different parts of the human body as a trust. The heart subtle center is located on the left side of the breast, two inches beneath the nipple. The spirit subtle center occupies the same position on the right side of the chest. The secret subtle center is on the same side as the heart, four inches above the heart subtle center. The hidden subtle center is on the right four inches above the spirit subtle center. The most hidden subtle center is located in the middle of the breast, between the heart and spirit subtle centers. The self subtle center is located on the forehead between the eyebrows. The location of the remaining four subtle centers, the gross elements, is in the physical form of the body.

At the same time, each of these subtle centers of consciousness is also related to the essential nature of one of the law-giving prophets (s): the heart subtle center is under the control of Prophet Adam (s); the spirit subtle center is under the control of Prophet Abraham (s); and the secret subtle center is under the control of Prophet Moses (s). The hidden subtle center is under the control of Prophet Jesus (s); and the most hidden subtle center is under the control of Prophet Muhammad (S). These five subtle centers of consciousness are in reality five stations of closeness to God, which one has to pass through to reach the Pure Essence of Reality.

Worldly relationships and desires displace these five subtle centers of the world of command from their original positions and they lose their illumination. The attention of the perfect shaykh restores them to their original position and they regain their light. The true form of each subtle center in the world of creation exists on the heavenly throne. Annihilation cannot be achieved until each subtle center reaches its true form. As the seeker progresses, they finally reach their true form and remain in God.

Hazrat Shah Wali'ullah (r) writes in his book *Altaf al-quds* (*The Most Subtle Sanctity*) that the science of subtle centers of consciousness is a great blessing that God bestowed on the later Sufis. After the Prophet Muhammad (S), prophethood came to an end yet aspects of prophethood still continued. Those who are graced with this status in their capacity as representatives of the Prophet renew the religion, for they have the authority to guide and purify people.

Hazrat Mazhar Jan-i Janan (r) (assas. 1781) writes that other than prophethood, no kind of perfection has fundamentally come to an end. The fountainhead of God's bounty knows no bounds. The blessings of God are infinite and are manifested in accordance with the capacity of every saint. God has bestowed miracles on those who came later out of His perfect and highest wisdom.

*

The purpose here has not been to demonstrate the superiority of one Sufi order over another. All Sufi orders lead to the final destination, and all of them more or less, have the same goal. However, it is clear that there is a difference in the methods with which the goal is achieved, because some paths are shorter allowing a shorter time to reach the destination and others are longer and take more hard work. This can be explained with reference to the mode of travel in the modern age. Consider traveling to the holy cities of Mecca and Medina. In the past, people had to travel for several months to reach their destination, now air travel has made it possible to reach Mecca within a few hours; the destination is the same but some reach it after several months and others after just a few hours.

Remembrance of God (*dhikr*)

Any act that is in keeping with the shari'a is a remembrance of God, even if it is buying and selling. Remembrance of God is commonly understood to mean the recitation and constant repetition of certain verses or phrases from the Holy Qur'an. The importance of the ritual has always been understood, as God commanded the Prophet Musa (s) to perform remembrance of God. In the terminology of Sufism, remembrance of God refers to the remembrance of the Name of the Essence (*dhikr-i ism-i dhat*), which involves the repetition of the word Allah and the remembrance of negation and affirmation (*dhikr-i nafi wa-ithbat*), *la illaha illa Allah* (There is no god but God). Shaykhs ask their disciples to practice remembrance of Allah so they can cleanse their inner beings. Remembrance of God involves both the tongue and thought, and in this way it is connected to both the outer and inner aspects of the human being. The objective of the daily practice is to establish inner and outer remembrance. The purpose of remembrance of God is to guard against forgetfulness and establish remembrance and an association with God. The obligations and commandments of religion are in reality the fruits of remembrance of God, and its practice makes human beings more keenly aware of their obligations and responsibilities.

There are many different ways of remembering God. In the time of the Prophet (S), the association with him, or even one glance from him, was sufficient to establish a remembrance of God. Later, when the different branches of inner knowledge and outer sciences were separately compiled, the shaykhs considered remembrance of God to be an important practice in Sufism. To establish remembrance, permanent awareness, and the perfections of the earlier saints, they devised a methodology for remembrance of God which took into consideration the environment of their times. Some emphasized silent remembrance of God (*dhikr-i khafi*), others vocal remembrance of God (*dhikr-i jali*), some the remembrance of negation and affirmation, while others emphasized remembrance of God's essential name. Some stand while others sit or lie down; some have special postures; and at times movement and activity is adopted to enhance the effect.

Wherever remembrance of God is enjoined in the Holy Qur'an it is more often than not qualified by the word 'abundance'. *Remember Allah often* (Qur'an 33:41); *and do not slacken in remembrance of Me* (Qur'an 20:42). As the purpose of abundant remembrance of God is never forgetting God, the person who has little 'forgetfulness' in life is one who does abundant remembrance of God. Shaykhs determine the number of times remembrance of God is to be done so that as progress is made, the state of never forgetting is achieved, and the seeker can experience the presence of God.

Hazrat often recited this couplet:

When I began thinking of Him, I could think of nothing else
Thoughts of Him obliterated all other thoughts from my heart

Remembrance of God itself is not a ritual nor is it like other rites. It is deeply connected to the purpose of life. Remembrance of God is an exalted psychological state that becomes part of a human being's consciousness (not merely a habit) and an integral part of that person's being. Just like the thought of a beloved you are separated from makes you ever restless, it is said that the one who remembers feels blessed, and otherwise feels ruined. As a result of remembrance of God it becomes easier to attain nearness and acceptance of God and achieve a higher spiritual awareness. The other benefits of *So remember Me. I remember you.* (Qur'an 2:152) are alertness, awareness, recognition of responsibilities, joy, consistency of action, the enlightenment of the self, and scaling the spiritual heights.

Remembrance of God also leads to the purification of thoughts. The degree to which human beings are trapped is such that it cannot be put into words. Usually the spirit is also imprisoned. Remembrance of God gives the human spirit the strength to ascend to great heights. One must do so much remembrance of God that no veils remain. Only *hu* remains.[7] One should renounce all hopes and desires and do remembrance of God with abundance, as the doors of one's inner being do not open without it.

When engaging in remembrance of God, the meaning of the recitation should be focused on completely. When one says *la illaha* (the negation), one should visualize the annihilation of the entire universe, and when one says *illa Allah* (the affirmation), one should focus on God as the goal and see Him as the Eternal Being until the unity of the phrase, "There is no god but Allah and Muhammad is His Prophet" is ingrained in the heart and the effects of remembrance of God become visible. The perfection of remembrance of God is that the heart of the person engaged in remembrance of God should be so immersed in God, that the seeker forgets even the word God. Finally, there is no distinction between the remembrance of God and the person doing the remembrance of God, for such practices are there to attain the overwhelming dominion of the love of God. At times the abundance of love is simply bestowed by God, but constant remembrance of God is obligatory on the Path.

Meditation (*muraqaba*)

The meaning of *muraqaba* is to detach oneself from worldly pursuits for a period of time with the intention of nurturing the spiritual guidance that the seeker has received from his shaykh. Another way of putting it is that in a human being's inner being there are subtle centers of consciousness. If, after receiving guidance, one takes time from worldly pursuits to focus on these subtle centers, then that is meditation. Meditation leads to inner knowledge and paves the path

7. *Hu* has a double meaning: "He is." and an abbreviated version of Alla<u>hu</u> signifying God.

to nearness with God. When the seeker detaches him or herself from other pursuits and sits and waits for blessings, sooner or later the seeker begins to feel some kind of activity in the heart, sometimes in the form of heat, sometimes as movement, and at other times as a tingling sensation. The seeker must not focus on the spiritual form or color of the heart, because the attention must be directed towards the Divine Essence, that is beyond all qualities. It is necessary to sit in meditation for at least thirty to forty-five minutes and no particular sitting posture is required. In the beginning, there is a rush of thoughts in the seeker's mind; this is no cause for concern. Hazrat used to say that we are not trying to concentrate our thoughts, as is the practice in yoga and other spiritual techniques. We are trying to awaken the heart.

Once the heart is awakened, thoughts gradually subside. Eventually the seeker experiences a drifting and enters a different dimension. There is a difference between this drifting and sleep. Drifting is the shadow of annihilation. Hazrat Shaykh Ahmad Faruqi Sirhindi (r) said, "He comes and He takes you away." In sleep, the soul is inclined towards the lower realm and takes refuge in the heart. In the state of drifting the soul is inclined towards the higher realm and takes refuge in the self (*nafs*). When the seeker is in the state of drifting, the seeker is not aware of individual being. In this state the seeker can also experience visions (*kashf*). As it is possible for the seeker to have thought projections, no importance should be attached to these experiences. Hazrat Shaykh Ahmad Faruqi Sirhindi (r) said, "These experiences are simply there to please the seeker's heart. The final destination lies ahead." Hazrat 'Ala'uddin 'Attar (r) (d. 1400) said that meditation is better than the practice of the remembrance of negation and affirmation. Through meditation it becomes possible to attain the station of viceregency of God in the dominion of the physical world and the world of spirit.

Awareness of the Heart (*waquf-i qalbi*)

In some Sufi orders, awareness of the breath (*pas anfas*) is practiced, and care is taken that God should be remembered with every breath. Instead of these practices, the Mujaddidis practice 'awareness of the heart'. The heart should remain aware and near to God. Remembrance of God is purifying oneself of forgetfulness. This cannot be achieved without awareness of the heart. The seeker has to protect the heart against distractions until nothing remains but God. The seeker should become so immersed in this practice that even if the seeker were to go to the market, they would hear no voices. When one is working one gets so involved in one's work that one becomes forgetful of God. This is why it is necessary for the seeker to focus on the heart and say 'Allah' at intervals, directing the attention towards the Divine Essence. When not remembering God, the seeker should direct the attention towards the heart and should be careful so that thoughts of all that is other than God can find no place. This will direct the seeker's attention towards God. As it is not possible for the heart to remain idle, the saints have said, "Keep the heart empty of the enemy and you will not need to seek the Beloved."

*

After explaining these key teaching methods and principles, we turn to the real subject of discussion. We have already mentioned that Hazrat Shaykh Ahmad Faruqi Sirhindi (r) revitalized the Naqshbandi teachings, creating a new path, the Naqshbandiyya-Mujaddidiyya. He made the path understandable and much easier for seekers to reach the final destination. In the same way, Hazrat Sayyid 'Abdul Bari Shah (r) modified the Mujaddidi path to an even greater extent by making it clearer, shorter, easier, and of benefit to the greatest number of people. Just as there is a curriculum for formal education, he devised a curriculum for spiritual training. He established certain rules and regulations to be observed by seekers so that they could travel with ease on the path of Divine love.

Considering the number of modifications that Hazrat Sayyid 'Abdul Bari Shah (r) made in the Naqshbandi-Mujaddidi practice, it appears as if a different path came into existence that could have been called the Mujaddidi Bari Shahiyya order.[8] However, because of Hazrat Sayyid 'Abdul Bari Shah's (r) extreme humility and his preference for self-effacement, Hazrat Hamid Hasan 'Alawi (r) did not think it appropriate to give it a new name. At first, in the *fatiha* recitation said after sunset prayer and the *khatm* recitation after the dawn prayer, blessings were offered to only the founder of the Mu-

---

8. I considered presenting a comparison between the practices of the Mujaddidiyya and those of Hazrat Sayyid Abdul Bari Shah (r) so that it could be shown how Hazrat Sayyid Abdul Bari Shah (r) had modified the Mujaddidi order to such an extent that, even though he did not give it a new name, his blessed being had created a new path. Due to shortage of space, this comparison has been omitted. Readers will be able to assess the differences for themselves from the ensuing detailed discussion of the teaching.

jaddidi path, Hazrat Shaykh Ahmad Faruqi Sirhindi (r). However, Hazrat Sayyid 'Abdul Bari Shah's deputies, Hazrat Hamid Hasan 'Alawi (r) and Hazrat 'Abdussamad (r), included his name in the *fatiha* and *khatm* recitations, and extended the practice of the *khatm* to other orders such as the Chishtiyya, in which this practice had not existed before.

According to the teachings which he received from his shaykh, Hazrat Hamid Hasan 'Alawi (r), who in turn received the teaching from Hazrat Sayyid 'Abdul Bari Shah (r), Hazrat Maulvi Muhammad Sa'id Khan Sahib (r) gave training to students in all the five major Sufi paths, according to the principle of 'the end is included in the beginning'. We will now try to explain the method of his teaching in some detail so that the wisdom and far-sightedness with which Hazrat taught students and guide them to the final destination can be seen.

It should be made clear however, that words are only the means for attaining true spiritual affinity. Spiritual transmission and affinity must be sought through shaykhs who have the authority to teach.

*

When a seeker would come to Hazrat for guidance, Hazrat tried to clear the doubts in the mind of the seeker before giving him or her the initial practices. He thought that even though people were becoming more inclined towards spirituality, to term this inclination spirituality was not always appropriate. Between materialism and spirituality there is the phenomenon of spiritualism, and this difference between spirituality and spiritualism is often overlooked. Spiritualism is to be found among those who have renounced materialism and its demands but who have no connection with the world of divine command. People endowed with spirituality are entirely different because they act in accordance with God's commandments, believe in His prophets (s), and live according to their guidance. As a result of this, acceptance and nearness to God is bestowed on them.

As Hazrat was interested in teaching seekers spirituality, he attempted in the very beginning to clarify the seeker's thoughts on this through an informal discussion. Hazrat spoke to each seeker according to each person's understanding and explained the aims and objects of the path of Sufism so that if the seeker were only interested in spiritualism, the seeker could go elsewhere and time would not be wasted. Hazrat wanted the seeker to decide for him or herself and did not take the initiative in the decision.

Hazrat said that to walk on this path and reach the final destination was not child's play, as it was a life-long project. You have to keep trying until your last breath, *And serve your Lord until what is certain [death] comes to you* (Qur'an 15:99). This is only possible if you make this path the raison d'être of your life. Actions are deeply related to one's aim. Without action a goal becomes meaningless and without a goal, action is futile. Life is, in essence, about action and without an aim there is no right action. Right action is that which flows from a noble and exalted goal, and we cannot think of a goal more exalted than the pleasure and acceptance of God. The task of the shaykh is to guide seekers towards the goal and instill enthusiasm and zeal in them.

Hazrat always ascertained before beginning the teaching if the seeker had already been initiated by another shaykh, and if that shaykh was still alive. If the shaykh were alive, Hazrat would ask him or her to develop that relationship. If the seeker still insisted on being initiated, he asked the person to get written permission from the other shaykh, always taking care to observe the rules and principles the elders had formulated on the basis of their experience. Usually, initiation is considered a pre-requisite for receiving the teaching. It is perhaps only in Hazrat's order that it is not necessary to be initiated in the beginning. Hazrat Sayyid 'Abdul Bari Shah (r) had wanted to do away with the tradition of initiation but from a spiritual point of view, initiation is considered to be necessary after the station of repentance. Without initiation the seeker can receive teaching up to the ten subtle centers of consciousness. During this period the shaykh and the seeker get a chance to understand each other and the seeker is mentally prepared to become initiated. The seeker will understand clearly that initiation is a contract between the shaykh and the seeker, assuring that the seeker knocks on one door and holds on to it. Without looking here and there, the seeker can progress towards the destination. During this time, the seeker also realizes that the relationship between the shaykh and the seeker is not just about becoming initiated and establishing a connection with the spiritual lineage. It is about staying in the company of the shaykh, receiving the teaching, and completing the training through consistent effort.

Hazrat said that as far as the seeker's etiquette or respect towards the shaykh is concerned, it is not a matter of rituals but a matter of the heart. As the seeker makes progress and the seeker's understanding and spiritual insight develops, the seeker can appreciate the spiritual status of their shaykh. Feelings of respect and awe develop in the seeker's heart, and they experience intense love for the shaykh, and their heart and mind are filled with deep, overwhelming gratitude.

*

There are two ways within Sufism: one is the path of divine attraction and the other is the path of spiritual practices. Depending on the seeker's natural inclination, Hazrat guided seekers on one of these paths or the other. In the state of divine attraction to God, the components of being are dissolved and the veils of Eternal Being are lifted. The inner being of the seeker is awakened with the help of divine attraction. The path of spiritual practices involves the seeker cultivating and immersing him or herself in spiritual affinities.

Once the student was mentally prepared and did two cycles of the prayer of repentance the teaching began. Although Hazrat imparted the teaching of all the major Sufi paths, the Mujaddidiyya was given preference because, for many reasons, it is easier for seekers to progress. However, if a seeker wanted to receive the teaching of say, the Chishti or Qadiri orders due to a family connection, or some other reason, the seeker was given the teaching in accordance with the seeker's wishes.

Recitations and the daily practices are arranged according to the timings of the five daily prayers so that a separate time does not have to be allocated and they can be completed after the completion of the prayers. Daily recitations and practices begin with the invocation of blessings on the Prophet (S) and his family. After the evening prayer one recites these invocations a certain number of times with a specific intention. When the blessings of love are received, a state of drifting and inebriation comes upon the seeker. It becomes difficult to complete the blessings of the Prophet (S) in this state of drifting. The seeker should spend forty-five minutes to an hour in this state and if the seeker has still not been able to complete the number, the recitation should be ended and considered complete.

Once the practice of the recitation of blessings on the Prophet (S) and his family has been established, the seeker is asked to begin the *fatiha* at the time of the sunset prayer and the *khatm* at the time of the dawn prayer. The *fatiha* is a recitation consisting of two specific chapters from the Holy Qur'an and the blessings on the Prophet

(S) and his family which are recited a certain number of times. The blessings of this recitation are offered to the founders of the order, Hazrat Sayyid 'Abdul Bari Shah (r) and all the others of the Mujaddidiyya. After this the seeker starts to do meditation. As far as the dawn *khatm-i sharif* is concerned, the blessings on the Prophet (S) and his family is recited in the beginning and at the end a certain number of times. In between, *la hawla wala quwwata illa billah* (there is no power other than Allah) is recited a certain number of times. The blessings of this recitation are offered to the pure souls of the founders of the order and Hazrat Sayyid 'Abdul Bari Shah (r). The recitations are then followed by meditation.

Along with these practices are those involving the subtle centers of consciousness belonging to the world of command. First the meditation of the heart is begun with a special intention. No recitation is required during the meditation. One only has to give up the activities of the external world and sit for some time paying attention towards God. Before starting the meditation, the following verse is recited once: *Ufawwidu amri ila Allah Inna Allaha basirun b'il 'ibad.* (I commit my own affair to Allah for Allah watches over His servants) (Qur'an 40:44). When one sits in meditation thoughts start rushing around in the head. The seeker does not need to worry about these because after awhile these thoughts subside and the seeker enters a state of drifting, another dimension. In this state the seeker has some experiences that are called visions. The seeker is expected not to give any importance to these visions. He or she should sit for at least half an hour to forty-five minutes everyday, without fail, so that the effects of blessings begin to manifest themselves on the heart. In this way, after perseverance in daily recitations, practices, meditation, receiving the shaykh's attention, and the blessings of God, the heart is awakened and is in a state of constant remembrance. This in itself is not less than a miracle. The seeker is then told to practice awareness of the heart. In addition the seeker is instructed to spare some time to engage in recitation of the Holy Qur'an each day, using a specific intention.

When by the grace of God, the effects of blessings are felt in the heart subtle center then the seeker is instructed to include the spirit subtle center with the heart subtle center. Once the effects of blessings are felt in the spirit subtle center, the secret subtle center is then included with heart and spirit subtle centers. In this way, one after another, the other subtle centers, i.e., the hidden, most hidden, self and the four elements are included. Once the ten subtle centers have been included, then a single intention is given for all ten. After some time, by the grace of God, the effects of remembrance of God become apparent in the ten subtle centers. If there is not sufficient light, then the meditation of the illumination of the subtle centers is given.

When the seeker reaches the sixth subtle center, the remembrance of negation and affirmation is assigned. A certain number is given, but if more purification is needed, then the number is increased. After completing the specified recitations, the seeker is told to hold the breath and say, 'There is no god but Allah' (*la illaha illa Allah*) twenty-one times and on the twenty-first time add, 'Muhammad is His messenger' (*Muhammadurrasul Allah*). If the prescribed number cannot be completed, it can be done any time before the afternoon prayer the next day. For this remembrance of God it is important for the stomach to be empty. Meditation after remembrance of God is encouraged.

Once all ten subtle centers are illuminated, the meditation of the station of repentance is given. Before this meditation is given, one has to be initiated. Although the teaching of one order is imparted initially, the seeker is initiated into all the major Sufi paths. Hazrat Sayyid 'Abdul Bari Shah (r) used to keep the seeker in the station of repentance for a long time. Hazrat, however, kept someone for a minimum of six months and a maximum of one and a half to two years. When the intention for the station of repentance is given, the seeker is also asked to recite the *durud-i siraj al-munir* a certain number of times. If there is need, the meditation of purification is assigned. During the meditation of the station of repentance, the seeker is asked to recite the following at intervals while focusing on the meaning of the verse; *Rabbana zalamna anfusana wa-in lam taghfir lana watarhamna la-nakunanna min al-khasirin*. Our Lord! We have wronged our own souls. If You do not forgive us and have mercy on us, we will be lost (Qur'an 7:23). The station of repentance is done only in the heart subtle center.

When, by the Grace of God, the station of repentance has been completed, then the meditation of the different circles of the subtle centers is assigned and the seeker undertakes a detailed journey.

*

First, the transmission of the circle of the heart subtle center, the first circle, the sphere of possibility, is assigned to the seeker. In this circle there are two arcs. In the first, there are two transmissions. In the center of the circle, there is one transmission and in the other half of the circle there are two transmissions.

The second circle is the sphere of the shadows. There are seven transmissions in this circle. The third circle, known as the sphere of lesser intimacy with God has two transmissions. In the fourth circle, the sphere of greater intimacy with God, there is only one transmission. Similarly, other than the four gross elements, the subtle centers of spirit, secret, hidden, most hidden, and self, like the heart subtle center, also consist of four circles. Seekers are asked to do meditation on the fifteen transmissions that each of these subtle centers contain. After the completion of the four circles of the self subtle center, the four transmissions above the self subtle center are assigned.

After the death of Hazrat Sayyid 'Abdul Bari Shah (r), Hazrat Hamid Hasan 'Alawi (r) was blessed with three further transmissions. With this, the training of the Mujaddidiyya is complete. After completing the teaching of one order, which usually takes seven to eight years, and is in itself a great achievement, the teaching of the other Sufi paths can be given. It is not essential that the seeker should receive the teaching of the other orders. However, if Hazrat thought that an aspirant had the required capacity, determination, and zeal, he then started teaching the person the remaining Sufi paths. This teaching, as in the Mujaddidiyya, is also based on the principle of 'the end is included in the beginning'. Just as in formal education, if you have an MA in one subject, you do not need to start from the beginning to do your MA in another and can complete it within two years. In the same way, depending on the capacity of the seeker, the teaching of the other orders was, and is, usually completed in a shorter time.

The location of the subtle centers is different in the other orders such as the Chishtiyya and Qadiriyya. The locations of the subtle centers in the Mujaddidiyya have been discussed earlier. In the Chishtiyya and Qadiriyya, the hidden subtle center is located in the middle of the eyebrows. The most hidden subtle center is in the center of the head, and the self subtle center in the middle of the chest. In these orders, one recites blessings on the Prophet (S) and his family after the evening prayer but the wording and the number of times it is recited is different. In the same way, the *fatiha* at the sunset prayer and the *khatm-i sharif* after the dawn prayer are the same, but the number of recitations of the two specific chapters from the Holy Qur'an and the blessings on the Prophet (S) and his family are different. In these orders, the vocal remembrance of negation and affirmation, the remembrance of God in five strokes, and the remembrance of God as *haziri, naziri, shahidi ma'i* (God is present, watching, witnessing and with me), start from the first day. All three kinds of remembrance of God have to be performed loudly a certain number of times after the pre-dawn prayer (*tahajjud*).

In the Qadiriyya, the four stroke remembrance of the name of the Essence is also performed a specified number of times. In the Chishtiyya and Qadiriyya, instead of awareness of the heart, awareness of the breath is practiced and included in the initial practices. In the Qadiriyya, *Allah* is said during inhalation and '*hu*' is focused upon during the exhalation. In the Chishtiyya, *la illaha* (there is no god) is said during the exhalation, and *illa Allah* (except God) during inhalation. In the Naqshbandiyya, the word *Allah* is focused on both during the exhalation, and the inhalation.

In the Chishtiyya and Qadiriyya, as in the Mujaddidiyya, the transmissions of the sphere of possibility are given after the completion of the station of repentance. However, the names of the transmissions are different. The second, third, and fourth circles contain the same number and kind of transmissions as there are in the Mujaddidiyya. In the other orders such as the Chishtiyya and Qadiriyya, like the Mujaddidiyya, there are four circles for every subtle center with the exception of the four gross elements (the subtle centers of earth, water, air and fire). Within these circles there are thirteen transmissions that are meditated upon. Once the four circles of the self subtle center have been completed, then the four affinities above the self subtle center are meditated upon. In the Shadhiliyya there is only the heart subtle center and the perfections of all the circles are experienced within it. In this order, blessings on the Prophet (S) and his family, meditation, and vocal remembrance of God are all performed while standing. The names of the circles are similar to those of the Qadiriyya.

As Hazrat 'Abdul Bari Shah (r) was a shaykh of the Naqshbandiyya-Mujaddidiyya order, he could combine different affinities, and combined the intention for all the affinities and several circles would be meditated upon together. Hazrat followed the same practice.

*

While traveling on the path, the seeker has different kinds of visions and experiences strange and attractive signs. The seeker is warned that these are simply there to please him or her. The Eternal Being cannot be comprehended in this world. Hazrat Khwaja Baha'uddin Naqshband (r) said, "Whatever can be seen or heard or known is all other than God." It should be negated with the word *la* (no) of the attestation of faith (*kalima*). The careful seeker does not get attached to experiences and keeps striving towards the final goal. The seeker is not concerned with the phenomena of the unseen or visions. Neither does the seeker get involved with special supplications and magic that are performed to develop personal spiritual powers, because those who focus on these kinds of practices get distracted from the path. Every transmission brings some trials with it, and the seeker must not lose heart. Through regular and punctual practice, the seeker can become the recipient of God's blessings and the prayers of the angels. The blessings of God are like unseen guests, and the seeker should be deeply grateful to them. According to Hazrat Hamid Hasan 'Alawi (r), the perfections of the circles constitute God's army and His unseen forces. Without the support of these forces, the fortress of the rebellious ego cannot be conquered. Without controlling the ego it is not possible to attain inner knowledge and nearness to God.

The seeker is expected to put aside one hour for spiritual practices after sunset prayer, one hour after the evening prayer and an hour each at the time before and after dawn prayers. This means that everyone will start their practice in the last part of the night, and will try to be regular and punctual in their practices. In this way a person's practice could take four hours, and at most, six hours a day. Whatever the circumstances, or however urgent the demands are on one's time, it is expected that no one will fail to perform the daily practices. Whenever a person has to choose between worldly affairs and spiritual practice, it is expected that, to the greatest extent possible, the aspirant will give priority to the practices, because this will make completing worldly tasks easier.

The seeker should not, however, think that by completing the training the seeker has achieved spiritual perfection. A person should consider now that the work of the course has been completed, that it will be easier to persevere so that God may accept him or her. Everyone is expected to persevere with the practices and wait patiently for God's blessings. The more effort one makes, the easier it will be to receive the blessings and the power and perfection of the transmissions will be manifested. Without doubt, effort leads to spiritual progress but in the final analysis, progress depends on God's beneficence and blessings. When the seeker is immersed in the mercy of God, the inner being is illuminated. States are transformed into stations and the seeker is honored with sainthood and the person becomes a friend of God. Once the person attains sainthood, he or she is endowed with God-consciousness and peace. With God's blessings, help, and grace, the aspirant may then also be asked to return to the world and serve creation. If the person is fortunate, then with the blessings of God, spiritual duties may also be assigned.

What then distinguishes someone who has attained sainthood after years of effort and struggle from an ordinary human being? Though it may be very difficult to describe the qualities of such a person, some aspects of that person's attributes and capacities are presented here for the reader. As far as that person's inner states and stations are concerned, they cannot be described. When the seeker is on the threshold of inner knowledge and is able to realize the Almighty, the seeker becomes speechless and has no desire to speak about her inner state. Even if the seeker wanted to, the limitations of language make it impossible to relate.

It is said that when the ego is annihilated and it undergoes a complete transformation, a new existence is bestowed upon him or her. Such a person is no longer ruled by the unruly ego and surrenders him or herself completely to God's will. The seeker is imbued with divine qualities, is able to control the desires, and does not say or do anything against the will of God. To such a person the Will of God is revealed. Such a person develops the power to affect and transform hearts and attain true wisdom while being blessed with the acceptance of prayers and being granted true dreams and visions. It is said that the Truth always accompanied Hazrat 'Umar (R), and similarly it can be said that the Truth always accompanies the friends of God.

Thousands of stars cannot chase away the darkness of night,
One sun rises and illuminates the world.

Dr. 'Allama Iqbal (d. 1930) has written poetry in praise of such human beings:

You make visible the secrets of a true believer,
The intensity of his days, the tenderness of his nights,

His elevated status, his lofty thoughts,
His intoxication, his passion, his humility, his pride.

The hand of the believer is the hand of God
Overpowering, resolver of difficulties, opener of doors,
He is of clay and of light,
Imbued with divine characteristics
Soaring beyond the two worlds.

Expecting little, aiming for the stars
Enchanting and charming
Gentle and soft in speech, ardent in his quest,
As pure in war as in peace,
At the center of the circle of truth.
In a universe that is ephemeral and illusory
Culmination of the intellect, fruition of love
Spirit of the universe.

Chapter Three

The Spread of Hazrat's Teachings in the West

Hazrat Maulvi Sa'id Khan Sahib (r) was blessed with infinite sensitivity and compassion, and his compassion was not limited to the followers of any particular faith or creed. Wherever he encountered tyranny, oppression, and injustice or saw people suffering, he was deeply affected. Pained by the impoverished state of the Muslims, and particularly by the inertia and the apathy of the youth, he said, "Our youth are the descendants of learned men and women who were concerned with the enlightenment of humanity. For how long will they remain in a state of oblivion? For how long will the descendants of those who were concerned with the Hereafter confine themselves to the material world and remain imprisoned within it?"

Hazrat was deeply attached to the Holy Qur'an. A careful study and reflection on the sacred text, combined with the alchemical spiritual supervision and guidance of Hazrat Hamid Hasan 'Alawi (r), led to the illumination of Hazrat's heart and mind. Hazrat became keenly aware that Islam was a universal religion that addressed all of humanity. By referring to God as Lord, and Sustainer of all the worlds, the Holy Qur'an had made it clear that God's nurturing providence encompasses all of creation. God's grace and bounty is not limited by race, creed, or color. Similarly, the Prophet's (S) compassion encompasses all of creation. God reveals in the Holy Qur'an: *We sent you as a mercy to the worlds* (21:107); and *Say, Oh people! I am Allah's Messenger to all of you* (7:158). It is evident from these Qur'anic verses that the blessed Prophet (S) has been sent as a prophet and mercy to all human beings. The love and compassion that Hazrat felt in the beginning for Muslims came to embrace all human beings. Loving all of God's creatures, comforting and consoling the poor, providing solace for the destitute and broken-hearted, became not only a way of life for Hazrat but also an integral part of his faith. He frequently quoted the following hadith of the Prophet (S), "All human beings are the family of God. The people who are dearest to God are those who treat his creatures the best."

Hazrat devoted his entire life to promoting this spirit of humanity. He met people of different faiths with great loving kindness, his love and compassion winning the hearts of non-Muslims and

Muslims alike. Hazrat felt that providing guidance to those who were not Muslims should be a greater priority because they had the greatest right to guidance. He said that if a person believes that all human beings are created by God, then it is incumbent on him or her to not only love the Creator, but also to love and care for God's creatures. If a person has no love for God's creatures, then there can be no truth in that person's claim of loving God. In this world, the worship of God is known through the love a human being has for all of God's creatures. He or she should seek to please God by serving and contributing towards the welfare of human beings. A person is not a true worshipper of God without loving human beings without distinction of race and religion. Rising above sectarian and racial biases, a person must see all of humanity as one.

Hazrat believed not only in the oneness of humanity, but also in the unity of all existence. A person endowed with unitary vision is not perplexed by the multiplicity of the universe because the person who experiences God knows that different forms are reflections of the effulgence of the One. Similarly, the apparent diversity of human beings as distinct individuals grouped in races and tribes does not contradict their essential unity. Hazrat regarded a single person as one unit and the community as another unit that consists of persons. Similarly, he thought that a nation is also an entity that consists of multiple communities. Humanity however, contains all nations within itself. Just as a person's piety is related to a person being a good member of the community, similarly, a virtuous community is one that is in harmony with the nation. An exemplary nation is one that is not at odds with the rest of the universe and is a beneficial part of all humanity.

In the same way, Hazrat emphasized that the Holy Qur'an is a sacred scripture, revealed not just for a particular sect or community but also as guidance for all human beings. It presents what should be humanity's fundamental philosophy - a philosophy that is universal, timeless, and unchanging. One may term the Qur'an the manifestation of the nature of God, or one may give it the name of religion, or understand it to be the human conscience itself. The prophets (s) and sages have been the articulators of this primordial human conscience. The Holy Qur'an was revealed to turn human beings' attention to its fundamental philosophy and principle: that all of humanity is one, irrespective of differences of gender, race, color, and creed:

> *He is the One who has sent His messenger with guidance and the religion of Truth to prevail over all other religions, however hateful it may be to those who do not recognize Allah.* (Qur'an 9:33)

This verse from the Holy Qur'an tells us that, of all religions, Islam presents a way that is the most sublime and the most comprehensive. It wishes to acquaint humanity with the most exalted philosophy. The Holy Qur'an urges us to accept the truth that all of humanity is, in reality, one tribe. Just as all humanity is one, so also is the whole universe one. The fountainhead of all that we see in existence is One. In this same way, the Prophet Muhammad (S) is a mercy for all the worlds and his love is not limited to any particular group.

*

In short, such was the expanse of Hazrat's heart and mind that the suffering of the world appeared to dwell in his heart. Any thoughts of personal grief or happiness were lost in his concern for the suffering and anguish of humanity. He constantly worried about how people could be rescued from anguish and helped to find peace and tranquility. Hazrat used to say, "In the present age, it has become difficult to contain the forces of materialism and instill ethical values. The crisis that this world is passing through is not limited to any particular religion or nation - it is global."

Why were we born? Why are we here and why one day will we leave? The extent to which the West has ignored these questions finds no parallel in any culture or society before this. Today people are without hope. They have not found the peace that they are looking for and their lives lack meaning. Yet, strangely, the proponents of this culture audaciously claim that this new era has brought human beings happiness, prosperity, and leisure. In the nineteenth century every western country dreamed of great prosperity and believed that the golden age was about to dawn. The French revolution paved the way for the passage of the "Declaration of the Rights of Man" and the United States constitution granted people the right to pursue happiness, liberty, and prosperity. Indeed, the dazzle of material wealth made it seem that the heralds of the new era were going to deliver on their promises. Yet things began to fall apart. International events soon revealed the hollowness of their claims.

The First World War and the destruction it brought in its wake shook those who had envisioned a golden age. However, instead of being embarrassed into accepting the flaws of their worldview, after peace was declared they went about making optimistic predictions about the future with a vengeance - the age of justice, peace, and prosperity was about to begin! Then followed the Second World War, a war even more terrible than the first. The progressive advocates of the new era did not learn from this, nor did they acknowledge that their claims had been proved baseless. The purely material foundations of atheistic philosophy had proved unsuccessful in bringing peace, happiness, and prosperity to humanity, but they were not ready to admit that they had been wrong. Instead of embracing spiritual and ethical values, the West began to dismantle whatever was left of the old order in the belief that this led to success in the future and peace and prosperity in the world.

There is no doubt that physics has helped human beings to take control of the material world, but the intellect that has helped to perform this miracle has been unsuccessful in helping human beings to understand their true nature and reason for being. In the West, the theory of evolution led people to believe more and more firmly that the human body represented the final stage of evolution; human life had reached perfection. Western philosophers and scientists from Hume to Einstein remained involved with the material world. The motivation behind their efforts was to purify research of subjectivity so that the true nature of reality revealed itself. In this way, by denying religion and spiritual intuition, people began to lose knowledge of their inner beings. The involvement with material realities has led to a lack of concern about this inner aspect. As human beings moved away from the belief in the oneness of existence, they were deprived of peace and contentment. Atheistic philosophies have bred increased emotions of jealousy and hatred, leading to people becoming unaware of their selves and unable to live with others in peace and harmony.

On reflection, one realizes that the fountainhead of the human soul is an Absolute Reality that elevates the soul. The human soul is in quest of a permanence that can only come through communication with this Absolute Reality. The human soul wants to escape from the limiting construct of time and enter the eternal so it can be blessed with eternal life. In the West, a reflection of this realization was to be seen in the work of the German philosopher Nietzsche, but western philosophy and science led him to abandon this path of inquiry. Now we see that modern physics and mathematics have themselves shattered the idols of materialism, and it has become possible for human beings to consider that the Absolute Reality is not material, but has to do with the self and the spirit.

*

Once, when Hazrat was staying with me in Delhi, I said to him, "People in search of Truth come and visit India from Europe and America to meet with *sadhus, rishis,* and *sants* to learn yoga and other such traditions, yet in a real sense, their search does not lead them to the last destination. They are not attracted to Muslim holy people and Sufis. They assume that the first condition for teaching is conversion to Islam. It is not easy to change one's religion because it affects one's entire life pattern. For seekers like them, an institute should be established in which converting to Islam is not a condition. They should be exposed to practices such as mediation so they can develop an understanding of this path. The choice of converting to Islam should be left to their discretion."

Hazrat's face lit up with a special smile. Hazrat, who had been reclining, sat upright and remarked, "Western thinkers are of the opinion that evolution has reached its peak in the material and physical world. In the future, evolution will take place in the mental and psychological spheres. The denial of spirituality is now seen as a proof of sheer ignorance in the educated circles of Europe. These days, intellectuals in the West are recognizing the need for spirituality. Many think that if humanity is to be saved, the sole means for the salvation of a person is for him or her to choose a purpose in life that transcends material concerns. To achieve success in life she or he has to search for ideals that are beyond materialism."

Hazrat then agreed with my suggestion and said, "It is true. There is a need to think of a way of working with these people so that we can work towards realizing God's promise to Hazrat Sayyid 'Abdul Bari Shah (r), that his teaching will spread from East to West." We discussed the name for the proposed institute, its aims, and the way it should work, for a long time. Hazrat urged me to outline a proposal for the institute as quickly as possible so that it could be reviewed, and work on its establishment begun as soon as possible.

After consulting with a professor of philosophy, the late Zafar Ahmad Siddiqi, a professor of psychology, the late Anwar Ansari in Aligarh, and some professors of Islamic Studies at Jamia Millia Islamia, I drafted a proposal and rationale. The following is an excerpt from that proposal:

> *The Institute strives to understand the essential nature of man, the universe, and man's relation to it in a way relevant to the time and circumstances of today. While material energy and discoveries can and should be utilized in the service of humanity, the main objective of the Institute is to discover the capabilities and potentialities of the human self, and their utilization for the benefit of humankind . . .*
>
> *The hidden power of the human self, which we are seeking to tap and utilize, is the power of love. It is this power that frees human beings from the bonds of narrow materialism and selfishness, and persuades them to observe tolerance, sympathetic regard, benevolence, and self-sacrifice towards others. It motivates, inspires, challenges, and satisfies. The understanding of the nature of the self and its hidden powers will be conducive to adjusting our attitudes and behavior to others, and to the universe as a whole. It will reveal to us the powerful inter-relatedness of the human existence of the universe, and will bring forth a creed of Universal brotherhood and unbounded love . . .*
>
> *Everyone who values a practice-based approach to inquiry, and has a genuine yearning for knowledge and wishes to understand the reality of life, is invited to try our technique irrespective of an individual's adherence to any philosophical creed or religion. It is suggested that any person who is interested in our work should come and stay with us for at least one week, observe, and test our techniques. Only after close observation and through practical experience, will a person be in a position to assess the true value of our work. However, those persons who are, at the moment unable to undertake the journey to Delhi and stay at our Institute, can acquaint themselves with our techniques through correspondence. We shall send them instructions for their guidance . . . The Institute does not aim at propounding or rationally explaining philosophical problems or theoretical creeds. It simply seeks to promote a Path purely of experience and actual practice...*

After reviewing the proposal, Hazrat wrote in reply:

My dear Azad Sahib,
Peace be upon you. *Al-hamdulillah,* I am well. I have studied your proposal and made the necessary changes. Most of us are aware to some degree of the dilemmas that the world is facing. In their own way people from every walk of life are striving to bring peace, justice, and order to the world. No one wants to see people suffering from discrimination, poverty, and injustice. People want these evils to be eradicated so that God's creatures may dwell in peace. Materialism, in its own way, has led to tremendous progress but it has failed to provide peace and tranquility. We are certain that the human spirit will attain true peace from the dissemination of the elevated values of spirituality. It is essential to revive the spiritual teachings and techniques of the Sufi lodges that have come down to us from a venerable spiritual order. To meet this need, I think that a center should be established in Delhi where seekers may benefit from the teaching without any discrimination.

This is my understanding, the rest I leave to you. Peace be upon you.

Muhammad Sa'id Khan
31st October 1975.

Initially, Hazrat thought that the Institute should be named 'Search for Divinity' but later 'The Institute of Search for Truth' was thought to be more appropriate and the foundation for the Institute was laid in 1975. The following passages explain in detail the three stages a seeker passes through to receive the teaching of the Institute. They chart the development of the Institute as an international School of Sufi Teaching with branches in many parts of the Western world.

*

The method of conveying the teaching of The Institute of Search for Truth was specifically formulated to impart knowledge and teachings to seekers belonging to Western countries. The School of Sufi Teaching was initiated as the vehicle with which the Institute could do this. The teaching of the School is transmitted in three stages, and the instructions concerning the transmissions on the ten subtle centers of consciousness have been compiled in the form of ten separate lessons. Relevant explanatory material pertaining to each lesson is distributed among the seekers as needed, so that by the time a seeker has received the transmissions for the ten subtle centers, the seeker acquires an understanding of the basic principles of the teaching: recitations; meditation; initiation; prophethood; and Islam.

Our teaching is based on Islamic Sufism. In the first and second stages, the seeker is not required to adopt any religious practice nor does the question of embracing a particular religion arise. The seeker is completely free in this respect because we think that spiritual insight is required to make decisions concerning religious and spiritual matters. We try to develop this insight in the individual so that the seeker is in a position to decide for him or herself. Nothing is imposed upon the seeker. However, when the seeker wishes and consents to proceed to the third stage, then the seeker is initiated and embraces Islam. The seeker is then given the teaching of the third stage. At this point it is important to stress that it is not possible to proceed to the third stage without Islam and faith. It is therefore essential at this point for the seeker to embrace Islam, and to participate in the weekly group meetings where all seekers gather to meditate and perform the recitations. As a member of The School of Sufi Teaching, the seeker will continue to attend group meetings with fellow seekers of all three stages. This is another form of being in the presence of the shaykh. Group meditation, where seekers at all three levels meditate together in peace and harmony, brings many rewards because seekers also benefit from each other's spiritual energy and are purified. When seekers return to their homes after the gathering they feel spiritually refreshed.

According to the Sufis, the mind is not the only center of consciousness in the human being because there are other subtle centers of which the heart is the most important. The heart is the locus of illuminations and can perceive the truth directly. For this to happen there is a condition; the heart has to be awakened. Now the question that arises is, how is the heart to be awakened or enlightened?

In our order we seek the help of a special kind of meditation. There is a fundamental difference between our meditation and the meditations of other systems. We do not attempt to work through concentrating the energy of the physical body at a single point as is done in other systems. In our order the meaning of meditation is to detach oneself from worldly activity, and for a period of time devote one's attention towards God.

*

In the first stage of the teaching, the seeker sits in meditation, turning the heart towards the Holy Essence by means of a specific intention. When we turn our attention towards someone, that person also turns her attention towards us. So if we sit and focus our attention exclusively towards God, then God, who is pure and free from all flaws, will turn to us. His bountiful grace will affect the seekers, and His light will inspire and enlighten them, illuminating their path. Eagerness will be created in the person's spirit to soar beyond the material realm to the dazzling splendor of the spiritual realm. There is nothing astonishing about this. An undeniable marvel of Islamic Sufism is that when a seeker sits in meditation, turning his attention towards God, blessings and bounties from the Holy Essence in the form of light flow from the divine realm and affect the seeker's inner being. Gradually, the entire body is transformed into light. The seeker then has the ability to perceive realities that lie beyond the reach of the mind and the seeker acquires a certainty that they have set out on the right path. A new vision of reality comes to the seeker and begins to influence her life and thoughts in positive ways, as aspects of the universe not accessible to the rational mind are revealed. In short, the most important feature of our method is that it leads people to the Truth, through the Truth.

The mental confusion, psychological problems, and social ills that human beings are currently confronting exist because people have lost their connection with the Truth. If people were to renew their relationship with God, then it would be possible to resolve any kind of problem, and society would be cleansed of its troubles. This is the reason that from the very first day we endeavor to establish a connection to the Holy Essence, the Creator of the Universe, through meditation. Gradually the seeker becomes alive to the Reality that there is a Supreme and Exalted Being who is the invisible force behind creation. It is He who sent the prophets (s) to guide humanity to show us the path so that human beings may know and attain nearness to their Creator. Thus we acquire values that are noble and virtuous. It is a sad fact that the mysteries of the heart have been so neglected and that there has been little effort devoted to knowing the vastness of its capacity.

When the seekers sit in meditation, they start drifting into a state in which they become unaware of the self and enter into another dimension. In this state, the seekers can see many things that in conventional terms are called visions. In other words, it may be said that an ordinary person's eye is only able to see those things that are before him or her, but there are also some eyes that are able to perceive the happenings and marvels that lie beyond these material veils as clearly as they are able to see the things that are in front of them. It is the Creator of the worlds who lifts the veils from their eyes and provides them with visions that the ordinary human eye is unable to perceive. All that exists is a marvel of His creation. It is through this spiritual insight and understanding that the seeker feels the need to establish a relationship with the Creator.

The regular practice of meditation sharpens inner vision, which brings about a natural change in the way the person thinks. Then the aspirant can see human nature and existence in true perspective. The person begins to view life and its challenges from a different angle, growing increasingly certain of the truth of the teachings and doubts disappear. It is hoped that the seeker will develop sufficient spiritual insight to experience God consciousness: an awareness of the presence, omnipotence, and oneness of God. In other words, we hope that everyone will directly experience the benefits and efficacy of this path. It is expected that the seeker's latent potential will blossom and the person will be released from mental and psychological anxieties and tensions.

*

The aim of the second stage is to nurture the seeker's newly awakened inner vision and to strengthen trust in the Supreme Being. The person can then realize the importance of the prophets (s) in approaching and attaining proximity to God. It also helps everyone to realize the need and benefits of initiating a formal relationship to the shaykh. In the second stage the teaching course continues with nine more lessons beyond the heart since there are nine other subtle centers of consciousness. At this stage, the transmissions of the nine subtle centers are completed. Along with the heart, the aspirant includes the spirit subtle center in the intention for the meditation. When signs of awakening are felt in the spirit subtle center, then the secret subtle center is included in the intention for the meditation together with the heart and spirit. Gradually, in a similar manner hidden, most hidden, soul, and the subtle centers of the four gross elements are also included in the intention. Finally the intention for the meditation includes all ten subtle centers. Along with the meditation, each is instructed to perform the other recitations of the order that include the recitations of blessings on the Prophet (S) and his family, *fatiha, khatm,* and remembrance of God.

On completing the ten lessons there is an extraordinary clarity in the persons's perception and insight. The persons's inner vision becomes even sharper. Yet the aspirant senses that the road to further progress is blocked making him or her despondent. The shaykh comes to the rescue of the seeker and explains that in order to progress to the higher stages, it is essential to attach oneself to a prophet (s) because a prophet (s) is the true fountainhead of God's beneficence and bounty. An ordinary person does not have the capacity to receive proper direct guidance and illumination from God and obtain enlightenment. On the one hand, the prophets directly receive Divine guidance from God, so that they may selflessly serve God's creatures and enable them to embrace the Truth. On the other hand, the prophets (s), through their own character, purify people and ennoble them. It is important for human beings to know that their creator is One and to realize that the messages and commandments sent through the prophets (s) are true. The nobility of the prophets (s) is a source of profound inspiration, beyond the apprehension of the common person who cannot even begin to conceive the purity and the joy that enraptures those who are connected to them.

Prophets (s) have been sent from time to time to guide human beings. There is a prophetic chain of succession. Since the Prophet Muhammad (S) is the final link in the chain and there will be no other prophet after him, it is necessary that we follow the path shown by him to arrive at the final stage. If we were living in the era of the Prophet Jesus (s) we would have followed him, but just as it became necessary to follow the Prophet Jesus (s) after the Prophet Moses (s), similarly after the Prophet Jesus (s) it became incumbent on us to devote ourselves to the way revealed to the Prophet Muhammad (S) so that we may reach the final destination.

Spiritual transmission and affinity must be sought through shaykhs who have the authority to teach. As far as initiating a formal relationship to a shaykh is concerned, it is usually the first condition for receiving the teaching among Sufis. Apparently, it is only in our order that it is possible to receive transmissions on the ten subtle centers of consciousness without being initiated by the shaykh. At this second stage, the shaykh and seeker have the opportunity to develop an understanding and a rapport. As they become closer, the seeker's heart inclines towards becoming initiated and spending more time in the presence of the shaykh. This leads to the seeker progressing further on the path.

The explanatory literature provided with each lesson for the student includes some selected essays on Islam so that prevalent misconceptions may be discussed and explained. If the seeker has any misunderstanding of, or hesitation about adopting Islamic Sufism, it may be addressed directly so that the seeker does not encounter problems in deciding about the future.

*

At the third stage the main objective is for the seeker to be initiated, so that the training can continue, thereby attaining the honor of embracing Islam and sincerely acknowledge the unity of God. By being initiated, people can wholeheartedly devote themselves to this pursuit with the utmost courage, determination, and steadfastness. Then they may, in the minimum period of time, succeed in being elevated to the station of sainthood. During the third stage the person's understanding and clarity of perception continues to develop. As one's inner vision deepens, each person is well able to ascertain how far each of the different paths to realization can take them. Only then is the seeker convinced of the efficacy and truth of the path.

Westerners usually feel nervous about being initiated because this involves surrendering oneself completely to the shaykh. The fears in the heart of the aspirant about this surrender disappear by the time she or he has completed the second stage, because each person realizes what it means to surrender oneself completely to one's shaykh and understands the importance of initiation in spiritual development. As far as changing one's religion is concerned, if a person is genuinely interested in something, such changes are not viewed as sacrifices but are seen as one of the conditions that are necessary for the attainment of one's goal. A person who is keen to reach the final destination accepts the most difficult challenges and hardships of the path. Such a person is prepared to make all the changes and adjustments that are needed for the realization of the desired aim.

Hence, in the third stage tremendous care is needed. If the aspirant appears to be satisfied with the second stage then no demands are imposed on him or her until the person feels completely prepared to proceed further. When the shaykh has carefully appraised the seeker from every aspect and has assessed that the person is truly prepared to continue learning, only then is he or she allowed to become initiated. By becoming initiated the seeker also embraces Islam. Although in the beginning some difficulties are encountered in following the sunna, this hurdle is also overcome gradually and easily through the accompaniment and careful supervision of the shaykh, and with the person's punctual and regular performance of the practices.

At the commencement of each stage the aspirant has to sign a contract in which the he or she confirms the commitment to engage in the practices of the particular allocated stage of the teachings. Although the contract for each stage is different, the following is indicative of all three:

> *Under all circumstances, I shall endeavor to sit in daily meditation for at least forty-five minutes for a minimum of six months during which I will keep the shaykh informed about my progress. I understand that the practices and methods given to me are for my own use and are not to be shared with others. I will study the supplementary material related to each lesson. I have read the fifteen rules of conduct for seekers. I accept them and will make every effort to follow the instructions stated in them. I will regularly participate in the weekly group meetings where seekers from all three stages meet and meditate at a specific place and time. I understand that the group meetings are an integral part of my training. If financial assistance is needed for the administration of the school I shall not hesitate to offer my support.*

*

During the period of the early development of The Institute of Search for Truth, a number of people came to see me from America and Britain. They met with me and started the practices. Gradually, through them, other people from abroad heard about the work of the Institute and began to come and see me in India to receive the teaching. During this period, I also traveled a number of times to America, Britain, and Australia to provide guidance to seekers. Within a short span of time, branches of The Institute of Search for Truth with the name of The School of Sufi Teaching were set up in many parts of the world. At present The Institute has established branches under the name of The School of Sufi Teaching in America, Britain, Canada, Brazil, Australia, Singapore, Italy, Malaysia, Poland, Ethiopia, Kyrgyzstan, and Germany. In each branch, a manager is appointed who sees to the organization of the meetings, carries on the work of the Institute and gives instructions to beginners.

In places such as Britain, America, Australia, Singapore, and Hong Kong where the language of instruction is English, communicating our method of training is straightforward, but since different languages are spoken in different countries, language can be an obstacle in conveying the teaching. Therefore, we train seekers of different nationalities so that they may impart the teaching of the order to other people in their respective countries using their own language. For example, Andre, who is Polish, acquired the training of the order from me in both Britain and Australia. After resettling in Poland, he set up a branch of the Institute, and with my permission, began the work of the order.

The seekers who came to meet me in Delhi from abroad in the early years of the Institute, had to find accommodation in hotels and it was difficult to find them a suitable place to stay. Now, by the grace of God, a Sufi lodge with modern facilities for Westerners has been built in the campus of The Institute of Search for Truth. Instead of staying in a hotel, friends from abroad can now stay at the Sufi lodge. Seekers and students usually visit during the winter season, and at a given time, people from different countries gather together with the shaykh and participate in a disciplined and carefully planned program, leaving the Sufi lodge after a period of ten to fifteen days.

By the grace of God, the sapling that Hazrat had planted, watered, and nurtured with his own hands is gradually blossoming into a tree. In foreign countries, The Institute of Search for Truth is serving as a beacon of light for seekers of the Truth. It is gaining recognition and seekers who come to India in search of Truth, now knock at the door of our Institute. Initially, there was a sense that foreigners were less inclined towards the Sufis but, praise be to God, this has changed. The responsibility that Hazrat had entrusted to me has to a certain extent been fulfilled.

May God accept this as an offering for the Hereafter.

Chapter Four
The Discourses

In a gathering at my residence in Delhi, someone recited the following couplet and asked Hazrat to explain it.

Thousands of God's devotees roam the wilderness in quest of Him,
I shall be the devotee of the one who loves the creatures of God.

Hazrat said, "A person can never attain to selflessness and total sincerity until the prime motive of work is earning the pleasure of God. If the primary motive is serving humanity, the community or the society, a person's actions will not be devoid of egoistic motives. The ego will certainly be involved in such an enterprise. Such a person begins to think of individual needs as everybody's needs. Undoubtedly, caring for human beings is a virtue, but the highest virtue is performing all actions for the sake of God and for the attainment of His pleasure."

*

In Ahmadabad, Rahim Miyan asked, "Why is it that despite every kind of effort, it takes a long time for some things to get done?"

Hazrat explained, "Such is God's way. With Him there is no haste. The work is done at the appointed time. The delay should not make the seeker anxious or despondent."

*

In Madras, Mr. 'Ubaidullah asked, "What does success on this path depend upon?"

Hazrat replied, "Personal effort and striving open the door to progress and make it easier to attain the goal, but the essential ingredient is the company of the shaykh. The more one can be in the presence of a person who has attained inner knowledge, the quicker the progress. A glance from the Prophet (S) was enough to endow a person with this awareness. Those who had the honor of being among the Companions (R) have a higher spiritual status than those who did not have this honor, so, the company of the shaykh is the fundamental thing. Effort and the practices however, do make the work easier."

*

In Delhi, Mr. 'Abdussattar said, "These days material prosperity is at its height. What will happen to spiritual progress? How will spirituality reach its height?"

Hazrat said, "Spirituality did not reach its height because people stopped after preparing a plan. They did not put the plan into action, and so the door of spirituality remained closed. The youth need to come forward and, like their predecessors, excel in this sphere as well."

*

In Azamgarh, Mr. Irshad asked, "What is the definition of knowledge?"

Hazrat replied, "Knowledge is the ability to distinguish clearly between what is true and what is false."

*

In Hyderabad, Mr. Karimuddin asked, "Why have the Sufi lodges fallen into such a miserable and destitute state?"

Hazrat said, "The main reason is that the capability of the successor [to the shaykh] was not taken into consideration. In appointing a deputy it is essential to keep that person's abilities in mind. Instead, the son was allowed to succeed the father even when he lacked the aptitude. Hazrat Hamid Hasan 'Alawi's (r) son, Baqar Bhai, wanted to be his successor since Hazrat Hamid Hasan 'Alawi (r) had told him that he had a right to the inheritance that had been passed down from his grandfather to his father. However, as far as the order was concerned the succession was dependent on the capacity of the heir, and it was given only to the one who was worthy of it."

*

In Ahmadabad, Mr. Zaynuddin asked, "How can we remove agitation and perplexity from the mind?"

Hazrat explained, "There are various forms of mental perplexity. If it is for self-improvement and involves good intentions and striving, then to rid oneself of that perplexity is a fundamental mistake. In the past, people began to place images in front of themselves to eliminate such perplexity. Perplexity can facilitate progress. Where there is complacency, progress is not possible. Allow the thoughts to flow, do not try and stop them. The heart is doing its own work, and the mind is doing its own. Human beings usually obey the dictates of their mind; this is a form of tyranny. The British were ruling over India by force. Then they left. Now the Indians, who are the legitimate rulers, are in power. Similarly, in the present age the mind is in power. In its place, the rule of the heart has to be established."

*

In Ahmadabad, Afzal Bhai said that he planned to do the Hajj that very year and asked if there were any specific recitations that he should perform there.

Hazrat responded, "You should concentrate on performing the circumambulation around the Ka'ba and perform the 'Umra before or after the pilgrimage because one cannot perform these two acts of worship anywhere else. Simply looking at the Ka'ba is itself an act of worship. In Medina, recite the blessings upon the Prophet (S) and his family in abundance."

*

In Ahmadabad, Habib Miyan asked, "When is a seeker able to transcend the material realm?"

Hazrat responded, "Our being is unique. The heart and spirit subtle centers belong to the world of divine command but have been enslaved by the self. When a person obtains freedom from this slavery, the seeker is able to progress spiritually. Once a person is freed from the bondage of the ego, transcending the material realm becomes easier and can be accomplished in a short period of time."

*

In Bangalore, 'Abdul Jabbar Sahib asked, "What are the meanings of the terms annihilation and subsistence?

Hazrat responded, "Every station has an annihilation and an abiding. To lose consciousness is annihilation, and to regain consciousness is subsistence. The exalted state is when a person loses consciousness of a separate self and remains conscious at the same time. *Never did I lose consciousness, nor did I gain it.* The example of Hazrat Abu Bakr as-Siddiq (R) is before us. The Prophet (S) said, that if someone wants to see a 'dead person walking', then that person should look at Abu Bakr (R). Hazrat Abu Bakr (R) had attained such a high state of self annihilation that even on kissing the forehead of the Prophet (S) soon after the Prophet (S) passed from this world, he was able to recite the following verse from the Holy Qur'an (3:144): *Muhammad is only a messenger like the messengers that have passed prior to him. If he dies or is killed, will you turn back on your heels? Whoever turns his back [on Allah] will not harm Allah at all. But Allah will reward the thankful.*

*

In Jaipur, 'Azmatullah Sahib asked, "What is meant by the progress of the spirit?"

Hazrat said, "What is meant by mental progress? Mental progress is about developing the inherent capacities of the mind. This is also true of the spirit; the progress of the spirit lies in awakening its potentiality. Moreover, the spirit, heart, and certain other subtle centers of consciousness belong to the world of divine command. Once a person is freed from the self, the seeker is then able to soar. Spirits ascend to their respective stations in accordance with aptitude and capacity."

*

In Ahmadabad, Jamaluddin Sahib asked, "Why is it that often when we seek something from God, it is not granted to us?"

Hazrat responded, "If God does not grant us something, it is not because of any miserliness on His part. This withholding is His supreme bounty. There is a gift in this very refusal to give, but it is only the sincere that are able to comprehend the grace in this withholding. *If you dislike them, you may dislike something in which Allah has placed a lot of good.* (Qur'an 4:19)

*

In Bangalore, Mahbub 'Ali Sahib asked, "How will world peace be established?"

Hazrat responded, "People make claims about establishing world peace and attaining salvation but their claims are baseless and merely politically motivated. The establishment of true and everlasting peace is beyond human capacity. The true purpose of human beings is to return to their primordial nature. As goodness and piety are intrinsic to a human being's primordial nature, people strive to be virtuous. If you are virtuous you will not quarrel with anyone because quarrels are found where there is a lack of virtue. The noblest exemplar of piety was Prophet (S). A human being needs to know God. A dog recognizes his master; it is a pity that a human being does not recognize his Creator. If a person attempts to know God the seeker will realize that God is both Lord and Creator, and the Provider of sustenance. If God is the Provider of sustenance then why should there be dishonesty in worldly affairs? Why should we not make integrity our goal?"

*

In Madras, Shadan Sahib asked, "How can religion be understood from a rational perspective?"

Hazrat responded, "Religion is the name of returning to the innate disposition of our primordial nature (*fitrat*). Religion is particularly concerned with Reality. It is a natural and straightforward path, one that is in accordance with our intrinsic nature. This path is wide and spacious, providing every kind of comfort and leaves no possibility for the traveler to lose the way. If one is aware of its boundaries and its expanse, and the ease that it offers, then religion cannot be termed difficult. When misplaced harshness and narrow mindedness vitiate the pleasant and congenial spirit of this path, there can be no room for joy and religion and the call to religion is turned into a cumbersome burden. Guidance from the intellect alone is insufficient for living life. The intellect is indigent and in need of revelation from God."

*

In Hyderabad, Muhammad Miyan said, "In this day and age, it has become difficult to differentiate between the lawful (*halal*) and the unlawful (*haram*). How can one protect oneself from that which is unlawful?"

Hazrat responded, "In former times, great emphasis was laid upon being mindful of the lawful and the unlawful. Those times were different. These days it has become very difficult to discern the finer points of what is lawful and what is unlawful. Therefore, consider that which is deemed lawful in the shari'a as lawful, and that which is prohibited as unlawful. Remain constant about this but do not delve into the intricacies. Even in this age we have a fair idea, for example, that unlawful earnings block the flow of divine blessings. Another aspect to consider is that if a person does not socialize with others, how will the teaching spread? If you refuse to eat at the house of a drunkard, then how will you help that person to reform? Beginners however, should be more cautious about whom they meet."

*

In Bandel, Mr. Mujib ur-Rahman asked, "What is the difference between miracles (*karamat*), prophetic miracles (*mu'jizat*), and visions (*kushuf*)?"

Hazrat responded, "When something out of the ordinary is seen by everyone, it is known as a miracle. Knowledge of events that are to occur in the future takes place through spiritual vision. The term for an out-of-the-ordinary event that manifests itself through the agency of a prophet (s) is a prophetic miracle.

*

In Bombay, Hajji Kitabullah Sahib asked, "Are all those extremely attracted to God (sing. *majdhub*) the same, or are there some differences among them?"

Hazrat explained, "There are two kinds of people attracted to God: those who are beginners and those who are at the final stage. The people who are advanced are in a state of sustained awareness, although the quality of their awareness is different. The beginners are unable to absorb the light. A little light, and they lose their senses and begin to wander around, for it is not always the heart that is illuminated. Due to the light, matters of the world are disclosed to them. When a decision takes place in the celestial realms, the angels of this realm then inform the inhabitants of the lower realm, and the ones attracted to God are entrusted with tasks. It is not good to have someone attracted to God either as a friend or as a foe; it is better to stay away from them. Spiritual perfection is not that a person becomes attracted to God. Perfection is when a person reaches the heights of attraction and still remains in one's senses. Once, when a person from our order lost his senses, Hazrat Sayyid 'Abdul Bari Shah's (r) spiritual attention restored his senses. Hazrat Sayyid 'Abdul Bari Shah (r) stated, "There is a difference between my path and other paths. In my path, a person does not lose his senses even though the state of attraction comes and goes." The state of attraction came upon Hazrat Sayyid 'Abdul Bari Shah (r) countless times in the span of an hour, and yet he always remained sober. Remaining sober is desirable but losing one's senses is not."

During his stay in Allahabad, Hazrat was quite close to Mitthan Shah, who was a person very attracted to God. Mitthan Shah told Hazrat to take up residence with Maula 'Ali in Calcutta and work there. Later, Hazrat Hamid Hasan 'Alawi (r) also sent Hazrat to Maula 'Ali. When Hazrat said that Mitthan Shah of Allahabad also spoke of Maula 'Ali, Hazrat Hamid Hasan 'Alawi (r) remarked, "See how sharp their vision is! I had thought of several places where you could stay in Calcutta but finally decided on Maula 'Ali." Just as when a lustful person sees a beautiful face and tries to possess it, similarly those who are attracted to God are able to spot a spiritual person from afar and will try to make that person like himself.

There is a difference between an imbalance of passion (*junun*) and attraction (*jadhba*). With the former, the heat generated through the different kinds of recitations creates an imbalance in the brain, which needs to be treated. Attraction is when the seeker is able to endure the light. As Hazrat Hamid Hasan 'Alawi (r) said, "It is like a camel trying to enter an anthill. If the capacity is limited it is necessary to develop it. Some people are not able to bear the affinity and start to flounder; others are able to contain it."

*

In Dhaka, Maulana Mukhlis ur-Rahman inquired, "Which is more important, the fear of God or the love of God?"

Hazrat responded, "Fear of God is the foundation, while progress is made through love. True love has no ulterior motive; it is selfless and purely for God."

*

In Chittagong, Mr. Abu Sa'd asked, "Is there any difference between a religious person and one who believes only in ethical values, or are they the same?"

Hazrat explained, "Some people consider belief in ethical values to be true religion. Such people have been influenced by European philosophy and do not have the right concept of God. How can the person who has faith in God and who believes in the Hereafter be the same as the one who merely does good deeds? The Arabs held a similar belief that was refuted by the Holy Qur'an (9:19): *Have you made providing water to the pilgrims and caring for the*

Sacred Mosque the same as having faith in Allah and the Last Day and striving for the cause of Allah? They are not equal in the sight of Allah.

*

In Tata Nagar, Haji Ihsan asked, "What are your views on understanding the meaning of the Holy Qur'an through interpretation based on the dictionary meaning of words?"

Hazrat responded, "There is a difference between the dictionary meaning and the technical meaning of words. Commandments have to be understood according to the technical, and not the literal, meaning of words. For example, the literal meaning of ritual prayer is to move or shake the lower part of the body. Therefore, it is wrong to try and understand the Holy Qur'an through the dictionary meanings of words."

*

In Azamgarh, Mr. 'Aziz ur-Rahman asked, "What needs to be taken into consideration in spreading the teachings?"

Hazrat responded, "Essentially, one should strive to reform one's self. When one is graced with divine acceptance, then people will be drawn to the order of their own accord. Otherwise, no matter how much communicating of the teaching is done, nothing is achieved. One should keep on trying because even the reformation of one person is a great treasure for the Hereafter."

*

In Purnia, Maulvi Nazir Ahmad asked, "What is the difference between sorcery and prophethood?"

Hazrat responded, "Sorcery, as opposed to prophethood, involves craft, incantations, and spells. Prophethood is a manifestation of Allah's power and is pure revelation."

*

In Jaipur, Mr. Muhammad 'Ali Sahib asked, "What is the difference between a Sufi and a non-Sufi?"

Hazrat responded, "It is possible for a person to attain nearness to God through following the sunna, but only a Sufi attains realization with a detailed knowledge of various stations. Therefore, one can say that the difference between a Sufi and non-Sufi is the difference between having detailed knowledge and having a synopsis."

*

In Udaipur, Mr. Muhammad Baksh asked, "Is it possible to bring together the followers of different religions on the same platform?"

Hazrat responded, "There are two aspects to religion: the beliefs and the practices. As far as beliefs are concerned, it is difficult to arrive at an agreement. For example, there are those who do not believe in God, so they and the polytheists will go separate ways. Therefore it is difficult to unite everyone. Nevertheless, if we look at the practices of religion, to some extent reconciliation is possible. Serving God's creatures is considered important in every religion. Similarly, every religion seeks to reform society and inculcate a high standard of morality in individuals. But what is one to do about differences in belief? The fundamental questions that people need to be asked are: what should be the basis of reforms? What is the purpose of serving creation? What is the objective – to please an individual, or satisfy the state?"

*

In Bandel, Maulvi 'Abdul Hakim Sahib said, "Would Hazrat be so kind as to shed some light on how one can attain the state of being oblivious to everything but God, and of being in a state of union with God?"

Hazrat said, "Human beings have been created to fulfill the obligations of creaturehood, to serve and worship the Creator and to turn to God with the totality of their being. This is possible only when one is oblivious to all that is other than God. Being oblivious to other than God means freeing oneself from the bondage of all that is other than God and serving God alone so that finally one is free, even of one's self. The impressions of all that is other than God should be totally erased from the mirror of the heart so there is no sensory or material connection with anything, and no desire left for anything but God. There should be no place in the imagination for any kind of desire, not even for the delight of the Hereafter or the pleasures of heaven. This happens only after complete annihilation which is linked to the illumination of the Pure Essence and is marked by the love of the Pure Essence."

At times, my keen sight pierced my heart and being itself
At times, it was entranced by the Ka'ba and Somnath.[1]
('Allama Iqbal)

*

In Hyderabad, Sayyid Ahmad Sahib said, "I have tried to understand the concepts of unity of being (*wahdat al-wujud*) and the unity of contemplative witnessing (*wahdat al-shuhud*) by reading books, but I have still not achieved any clarity. I would be most grateful if you could explain these concepts in simple words."

Hazrat responded, "Hazrat Ibn al-'Arabi (r) presented the basis of what was later known as the unity of being. Sufis accepted him as their spiritual leader and this doctrine influenced Sufi thought deeply. This concept is very abstruse and therefore not easy to understand or explain. There is no need to delve into its complexities. A simple way to understand the difference between the unity of being and the unity of contemplative witnessing is that one is a state, and the other a station. A more detailed explanation is that everything that exists has being in common. Therefore, if there were no being, nothing would exist. Everything that is to be found in this universe other than being is contingent. If there were no being, nothing would exist. Therefore, being is nothing but the Divine Essence. The reality of all that exists in this world is this being. All things have emanated from this one Being and all this profusion of phenomena is Its manifestation. The individual attributes of phenomena (other than being itself) are conditional. Even people endowed with ordinary intelligence can comprehend this.

The Chishtis have been greatly influenced by the philosophy of the unity of being. This is why the propagation of this teaching has had such remarkable success in India. An incorrect interpretation of the doctrine of the unity of being resulted in excesses during the reign of the Mughal Emperor Akbar, including the custom of ridiculing of the shari'a, which became part of the religion of the court. Hazrat Shaykh Ahmad Faruqi Sirhindi (r) came to rectify this error.

In the beginning, Hazrat Shaykh Ahmad Faruqi Sirhindi (r) was a believer in the unity of being, but later spoke against these ideas. He said that it is wrong to think of the unity of being that we perceive in this world as the True Being. The Reality of Being lies

1. Somnath is a Hindu temple in the state of Gujarat, India.

beyond this. God is beyond our concept of beyond, and this universe is His creation. He existed when this universe did not and that is why this universe and God's Being cannot be the same. One is the Creator and the other is His creation. One is the Lord, the other His creature. Hazrat Shaykh Ahmad Faruqi Sirhindi (r) presented the unity of contemplative witnessing to repudiate the ideas of unity of being. The unity of contemplative witnessing affirms the unity and uniqueness of God whereas in the unity of being, God can be found in physical phenomena. Hazrat Shah Wali'ullah (r) has tried very beautifully to reconcile the two doctrines and is of the opinion that there is no real difference between the two, the difference being only semantic."

*

In Orissa, Jan Muhammad Sahib asked, "What is the difference between Islamic Law and the Sufi path?"

Hazrat responded, "They are inseparable. The observance of the laws of shari'a affects the inner being. Ablution is performed to cleanse the heart. Similarly the purification of the heart and the self makes it easier to obey the laws of the shari'a with awe and humility. No matter how spiritually advanced a person may be, that person is not exempted from the five daily ritual prayers. The people who profess to follow the Sufi path and claim that they have nothing to do with the shari'a are in the wrong. Hazrat Shah Wali'ullah (r) himself received divine inspiration that he could be exempted from obligatory observances such as the five daily prayers, but he prayed, 'O Lord, these are dear to me, so do not exempt me from fulfilling these commandments.' Exemption from the obligatory practices implied that he was not obliged to remain in a state of sobriety."

*

In Mecca, Junaydi Sahib asked, "What form do the practices take in your order?"

Hazrat answered, "In our order we do not have the austere practices of former times such as the upside-down forty-day retreat (*chilla-yi ma'kusa*) or prayers performed for forty nights where a person hung upside down from a tree into a well. We practice meditation which involves reciting a special intention and waiting for blessings. The more time one spends in meditation, the easier it is to traverse the spiritual stations. In our order, all the degrees of spiritual perfection are attained through meditation. Two things are important: regularity and punctuality. Consider it a duty to do the spiritual practices at the appointed time. Other than this, the company of those who are near to God makes progress easier."

*

In Dhaka, Maulana Mukhlis ur-Rahman said, "These days some people consider etiquette and good conduct to be sufficient and feel that there is no need for the obligatory ritual prayer. "

Hazrat responded, "It depends on what your objective is. If the aim is simply to be humane, then etiquette and good conduct are sufficient. However, if one is convinced of the existence of life after death, then along with respect and kindness for others, there is a need to develop a connection with God. The great error in this outlook is that it does not provide for a relationship with God, and as a result, there is no fear of accountability. This makes human beings reckless. On the other hand, in living a life that is connected with God, people know that if they do not fulfill their responsibilities towards others, they shall be called to account. The real purpose of the obligatory ritual prayers and fasting is piety and God consciousness, although there are other benefits such as increased sensitivity and the ability to encounter joy, suffering, and hardships with equanimity."

*

In Dhaka, Mr. Mahmudullah, asked, "It is commonly said that the devil is the shaykh of the person who does not have a shaykh. What does this mean? Is it necessary that every person should be initiated by a shaykh?"

Hazrat explained, "The popular belief that everyone has to become the disciple of a shaykh is absolutely wrong. Yes, if someone wants to journey along the Sufi path and wants to develop a relationship with the saints, then it is necessary for such a person to have a guide. One should not indulge in spiritual practices or recitations by oneself. In such a situation there is the apprehension of being deluded by the devil and becoming his follower."

*

In Hyderabad, Muhammad Miyan asked, "What are the differences between vocal remembrance of God, silent remembrance of God, remembrance of God through negation and affirmation, and remembrance of the name of the Essence?"

Hazrat responded, "Vocal remembrance of God increases one's yearning and the heart finds peace in the Name of God. The evil whispering of the self is silenced and it ignites a strong desire to give precedence to God over all that is other than God. Silent remembrance of God increases love and longing for God. It inspires courage, increases yearning, and instills sweetness in the heart and repugnance for all that is other than God. In addition to this, vocal remembrance of God exercises a pull towards the upper door of the heart and silent remembrance of God attracts the lower door of the heart. Remembrance of God through negation and affirmation is more beneficial for the spiritual journey, and remembrance of the name of the Essence is more beneficial for attraction. The former Naqshbandis did not possess remembrance of the name of the Essence probably because it was introduced by Hazrat Khwaja Baqibillah (r) (d. 1603 Delhi, India) or one of his contemporaries."

*

During a stay in Ahmadabad, Yusuf Miyan asked, "What is the difference between the recitations of the 'virtuous' and the recitations of those who are described as being 'drawn close unto God'?"

To this Hazrat replied, "There are two categories of Muslims: those who are 'drawn close unto God' and the 'virtuous'. The Holy Qur'an mentions these groups as well: *And the foremost of the foremost will be those nearest to Allah* (56:10-11)*; and let us die in the company of the righteous* (3:193). Every Muslim is among the 'virtuous', but those who are 'drawn close unto God' are among the elect. The main objective of travel along the Sufi path is for the 'virtuous' to be raised to the status of those who are 'drawn close unto God'. The actions of an ordinary Muslim are egocentric, and are motivated by the desire for rewards. Contrary to this, the actions of the elect are free from any impurity. In addition to being blessed with the rewards that they merit for their virtuous deeds, nearness to God is also bestowed upon them. Perfect sincerity is not possible for a person who has not attained the annihilation of the heart and extinction of the ego. Only when a person strives for both divine rewards and divine proximity will one's actions and remembrance of God be that of those who are 'drawn close unto God'. In the eyes of those drawn close to God, good deeds that are not motivated by an ardent desire to draw closer to God are thought of as a sin. There is a saying: that which the 'virtuous' consider virtue, those who are 'drawn close unto God' regard as a sin."

*

In Bangalore, Maulana Yusuf Sharqi Sahib asked, "How far can the seeker progress through remembering God?"

Hazrat replied, "Remembrance of God takes the seeker to the stage of extinction of the ego. Beyond this progress is achieved through meditation. Beyond this, there comes a stage when progress does not take place either through remembrance of God or meditation but is entirely dependent upon the grace of God. After complete annihilation, nearness is attained through supererogatory prayer. Then there is the stage where a seeker draws closer through the performance of specially assigned obligatory duties, which is the station of subsistence in God. This means that before, a person could offer any prayers as supererogatory prayer; in this stage, the seeker is assigned certain tasks by Allah and progress is wholly dependent on carrying out these tasks. If such a person does not perform these tasks and starts engaging in supererogatory prayers, the seeker incurs God's displeasure."

*

In Delhi, Aftab Sahib asked, "Does one receive the same benefits from the recitation of the Holy Qur'an as one does from the recitation of the blessings on the Prophet (S) and his family, and other special remembrances of God prescribed by the Sufis?"

To this Hazrat replied, "Each recitation has its own distinct qualities. The recitation of the Holy Qur'an has its own particular effects and other kinds of remembrance of God have their particular effects. During the initial stages abundant remembrance of God is required for the progress of the seeker. After attaining the stage of annihilation of the heart and annihilation of the self, recitation of the Holy Qur'an, supererogatory prayers, and other religious practices continue to facilitate progress until the heart is connected to the Creator. When a person is no longer subservient to desires and is free of them, this is called extinction of the ego. Now, whatever the seeker does will be done to please God, and therefore every action will further individual progress. It is said that after annihilation of the self, the seeker's being is annihilated and that the seeker is given another special kind of existence. This means that the domination of the lower carnal self that incites to evil (*nafs-i ammara*) ends, and the person becomes totally obedient to the commandments of God."

*

In Bangalore, 'Abdul Qadir Sahib asked, "What is the difference between our meditation and the yogic meditation? They appear to be similar."

To this Hazrat replied, "In Sufism something is received spontaneously. Suppose somebody is blind and has no concept of light, and then all of a sudden through an operation or through some other means, the seeker can suddenly see. This is Sufism. Without any projection or effort, something is received. In yoga thoughts have to be controlled, and something has to be developed through concentration, which involves effort. Where imagination and concentration of thoughts have a role to play, you cannot go beyond the material realm. Sufism lies beyond imagination and superstition. The truths that the Sufis have experienced leave little room for doubt. If there is any truth in the obligatory ritual prayer, then the understanding and insight gained through it shall be true. The practices of Islamic Sufism are truly for the progress and benefit of the seeker. God is free from all needs. We wish to gain insight and to awaken our innate potential. The Truth cannot be attained through superstition."

> *No human being can communicate with Allah except through inspiration, from behind a barrier, or by sending a Messenger through whom He reveals what He wills.* (Qur'an 42:51)

"If one knows and feels that something is being received, that is the Truth. The Prophet (S) did not go into the cave with any preconceived notion. When the angel Gabriel (s) arrived, the Prophet (S) was startled. Truth will be disclosed to some in ten years, to others in a year, and again to others in just a day. Some people have attained it through the help of human beings with purified souls and others through their own efforts, which took several years."

*

In Chittagong, Sufi Abu Sa'd Sahib asked, "Is creation the gift of a Benefactor or is it the result of an arbitrary accident?"

Hazrat said, "This is a debate which has been the subject of much hair-splitting. At the same time some light has also been shed on the reality of Creation - it is the gift and blessing of God. It is not meaningless or in vain. It has been brought into existence for a special and exalted purpose. The principles and resources to achieve this purpose have also been provided with the utmost care."

*

In Mangarawan, 'Abdul Wahhab Sahib said, "Religion is being spread in different ways. Which way do you consider to be the best?"

Hazrat replied, "As people are engaged in spreading religion in their own ways, they are equally admirable. Someone is engaged in giving lessons on the hadith, another in publishing a religious periodical, and yet another is occupied in some other kind of religious work."

*

In Chittagong, Hajji 'Ibadullah asked, "What should seekers be particularly mindful of to facilitate inward progress?"

Hazrat said, "A seeker should be mindful of performing spiritual practices. These should not be missed. The other important thing is punctuality. One aspect of this is that every effort should be made to perform the five practices that are essential in our order, namely, reciting blessings on the Prophet (S) and his family, saying the *fatiha* after the sunset prayer, and the reciting the *khatm* at dawn, remembrance of God and meditation, and awareness of the heart at the designated time. Secondly, attempt to remain constant in the practices. Apart from the appointed times, at other times practice awareness of breath and awareness of the heart so that the state of having one's hands engaged in work while one's heart is with the Beloved can be attained."

*

During Hazrat's stay in Delhi, Jamil Sahib asked, "Could you please suggest something to recite when I am not engaged in any work and would like to recite something?"

Hazrat said, "Do not be neglectful of remembering God and read the couplet of Jigar Muradabadi."

Once I thought of Him, remembrance did not cease
Effacing every image other than His.

(Jigar Muradabadi)

*

In Hyderabad, Maulana Karamat 'Ali asked, "What is the basic philosophy of Hazrat Shaykh Ahmad Faruqi Sirhindi (r)?"

Hazrat said, "Hazrat Shaykh Ahmad Faruqi Sirhindi's (r) basic philosophy is about establishing the kind of relationship with Allah that has been specified in the Holy Qur'an and the hadith. According to him, intelligence alone cannot lead to enlightenment because intelligence needs the light of revelation to illuminate the way."

*

During Hazrat's stay in Madras, Bashu Bhai said, "Sometimes, while doing the practices the student has experiences in which various other saints come to his aid. This causes the student to entertain doubts about his own shaykh. How should this be dealt with?"

Hazrat replied, "According to Hazrat Shaykh Ahmad Faruqi Sirhindi (r), the shaykh's subtle centers of consciousness can assume the form of the shaykh or that of other saints, and come to the aid of the disciple. Sometimes the shaykh is aware of this and at other times he is not. Nevertheless, the disciple should focus his attention solely on his own shaykh, and in order to make progress on this path, the seeker should be keenly aware of her own shortcomings, and be grateful to Allah for His bounty."

*

In Patna, Mr. Salahuddin asked, "What is the best way to preach Islam?"

Hazrat replied, "There are two aspects to the preaching of Islam. One is the inner way and the other is the external or outer way. The inner way involves trying to make someone who is already a Muslim a true believer. The external way involves developing sincerity in one's actions and purity in one's heart and soul, and cultivating a character that people of different faiths are impressed by and want to emulate by accepting Islam."

*

In Aligarh, a student asked, "What is the subject of Sufism?"

Hazrat replied, "Sufism is about the essence of human beings. There are many treasures hidden within a human being. Sufi practices help to develop spiritual insight and enable one to delve into the treasures of knowledge and wisdom hidden within the human being and the universe."

*

In Bhopal, Mr. Arshad said, "Some Sufis of the Naqshbandiyya are of the view that theirpath does not contain any prescribed recitations. To what extent is this true?"

Hazrat replied, "The practice of recitations in the morning, evening, and before going to sleep, has been authenticated by hadith and therefore it is not possible that Hazrat Khwaja Baha'uddin Naqshband (r) would have rejected them. However, later Sufis have added a lot of recitations that were not mentioned in the famous and authentic hadith. Hazrat Baha'uddin (r) avoided these and only included those that were part of the Prophet's (S) way. Hazrat Baha'uddin (r) has said that, 'The foundation of our order is following the hadith and the way of the Companions (R).'"

*

In Mysore, Mr. Amjad 'Ali asked, "In Sufism, there are so many practices and prayers. What is the reason for this?"

Hazrat replied, "We cannot say anything about others, but this is not true of our path. We do not preach or give sermons. We do however, place great emphasis on meditation and remembrance of God, since this practice of vigilance leads to the strengthening of spiritual powers and the weakening, and eventual disappearance of vice."

*

In Purnia, Mr. Habib Ahmad asked, "What should a seeker do after he has received all the transmissions? Are we then to consider him or her a saint?"

Hazrat replied, "The completion of the affinities or transmissions does not mean that there is nothing more to do. It simply means that the course of study has been completed. The time has come for the individual to work hard and to persevere in the practices. The harder the seeker works, the greater the spiritual advancement will be. One must continue to strive until the very end, *and serve your Lord until what is certain [death] comes to you* (Qur'an 15:99). The completion of the affinities does not automatically bestow sainthood on an individual. Only someone with spiritual discernment can evaluate a person's spiritual status. The student is like a patient whose job is to take the prescribed medicine. Yet it is up to the doctor to determine whether the medicine is having the desired effect."

*

In Tata Nagar, Hajji Nisar asked the following question; "What can a seeker do to increase his desire and commitment to the path?"

Hazrat replied, "The best way to increase desire and commitment is to spend time in the company of saints and seekers of divine knowledge." He then recited a verse from Rumi's *Mathnawi*, 'Sit in the company of saints and, if nothing else, you will develop a longing.' Once the veils are lifted from the heart, one's entire perspective changes. Hazrat 'Umar (R) left his house with the intention of assassinating Hazrat Muhammad (S), but when he arrived in his presence his intention was transformed and he accepted Islam. His entire outlook changed. Where he had once seen merely the son of 'Abdullah, he now saw the Prophet (S) of Islam. Guidance can come only from Allah and thus although Abu Jahal also beheld the Prophet (S), he remained unaffected."

*

In Bombay, Seth Ishaq asked Hazrat, "Many people say that daily practices can make one go mad. Is there any truth in this belief?"

Hazrat replied, "If a doctor prescribes two spoons of a medicine and the patient takes eight, his health will be adversely affected. In the same way, reciting more than the prescribed number of recitations or performing prayers for a specific purpose without obtaining the shaykh's permission can have a negative effect on the mind. However, it is perfectly safe to perform the daily recitations and practices that have been assigned by the shaykh."

*

In Orissa, Mr. Fazal 'Ali asked, "What is the difference between the knowledge of the self and the knowledge of the heart?"

Hazrat said, "There are two kinds of knowledge. The first is a product of the human ego associated with the soul subtle center. Medicine and philosophy are examples of this kind of knowledge. The second is knowledge that comes from one's inner being or heart, and is related to Allah. All the revealed scriptures and religions arise from the knowledge of the heart. The knowledge given to us by the Prophet (S) through the Holy Qur'an is the most exalted form of knowledge of the heart. A person who remains true to this knowledge will not be condemned if it is expedient to be involved in worldly affairs and financial or political matters. This is because the true purpose is to call people to the path of virtue."

*

In Bangalore, Mr. 'Abdul Ghaffar asked Hazrat, "What is the importance of Sufi practices?"

Hazrat replied, "When people asked the Prophet (S) if they should perform any other prayers besides the obligatory prayers, the Prophet (S) replied that it was up to the individual's desire and level of commitment. Thus while the observance of the five pillars of faith is considered sufficient for all Muslims, additional prayers and practices are for who have higher aspirations.[2] Such people are similar to the university student whose thirst for knowledge is such that the student reads much more than the prescribed syllabus. A child and a learned man or woman may both recite *surah al-fatihah* (the opening chapter of the Holy Qur'an), but there is a world of difference in their understanding. In the same way there are different degrees of faith. Sufi practices are designed to take one's faith to a higher level. There is a difference between ordinary Islam and true faith.

> *The Bedouin say, "We believe." Say [to them]: 'You do not have faith. Instead say, "We have submitted," since faith has not yet entered your hearts.* (Qur'an 49:14)

This verse indicates that there is something that enters the heart. The practices are there to ensure that faith does enter the heart.

Sufi practices were not needed at the time of the Prophet (S), because one glance from him was enough. The perfection of his spiritual powers was such that his teaching was enough to reform the hearts of his Companions (R). The most heinous infidels reached the exalted spiritual status of doing what is beautiful as soon as they recited the attestation of faith. These spiritual powers were passed

---

2. The five pillars are: Saying with one's tongue and in one's heart: "There is no god but Allah and Muhammad is His prophet, ritual prayer five times a day, paying alms, fasting during the month of Ramadan, and if possible, going on the pilgrimage to Mecca.

on by the Prophet (S) to the Companions (R), and from them to their followers and then their descendants, but each time in a more diminished form. Eventually the powers were so diminished that Sufi practices had to be initiated to address the deficiency. It became necessary to take help from practices such as meditation, vocal remembrance of God, and awareness of breath. The shari'a commands us to achieve the state of doing what is beautiful and to purify the self. Since no method has been specified for achieving these objectives, any method can be adopted. This method will not be part of the religion, but a means to religion."

*

In Ahmadabad, Mr. Zaynuddin asked, "What should we be thinking while we are reciting the attestation of faith (There is no god but Allah and Muhammad is His prophet)?"

Hazrat replied, "You should be thinking there is no God, no purpose and no being, no one worthy of being worshipped. There is no God but Allah. We negate all deities but Allah. We are not concerned with the translation or the meaning. Whatever concept there is of a god, we negate it."

*

In Delhi, Imam 'Abbas asked, "Should one focus on the action or its reward?"

Hazrat replied, "Great people focus on the action and not on the reward. One should not be upset if one does not get the result one desires. The main purpose is to continue with the work. God, however, has no need of our work and only he has the power to bestow guidance. (said to Muhammad), *You do not guide those whom you like, but Allah guides those whom He wills* (Qur'an 28:56). There should be great desire but no despondency. *No person knows what is waiting for him as a reward for his (good) deeds.* (Qur'an 32:17)

*

In Delhi, Mr. Rashid Ahmad asked, "Why is it that we have achieved so much worldly prosperity but have lagged behind in spirituality?"

Hazrat replied, "Success depends on endeavor. The harder you work the more successful you will be. *We will guide those who strive in Our cause to Our paths. Allah is with those who do good* (Qur'an

29:69). We have made so much progress in the material world that man has reached the moon. However, we have made little progress spiritually. Great effort is required to create something new and to achieve progress. It is due to hard work that nations prosper. This is the law of nature. We have been ruined because of our lack of effort. Take some examples from the world around us. The farmer toils on his land and Allah rewards him with the fruit of his labor. However, we are not willing to forsake even ten minutes of our sleep. If the commander is not alert, how will the organization function? Our youth need to work hard and then they will find their time more productively spent and will keep better health. Hazrat Hamid Hasan 'Alawi (r) is a perfect example. An ordinary person would have considered him to be more knowledgeable about agriculture than any other person. Yet, on the other hand, a person of spiritual discernment would be awed by his exalted spiritual station. Running away when confronted with hardship is not appropriate because challenges provide us with invaluable opportunities."

*

In Pune, Mr. 'Abdul Ghani asked, "What is the meaning of the phrase, 'Die before you die'?"

Hazrat explained, "What happens when a person dies? His relationship with this world ends. Before death comes, let the world hold no attraction for you."

*

In Ringhaloo, Orissa, Mr. Hardu Muhammad asked, "Why do the majority of the Sufi orders trace their origins to Hazrat 'Ali (R)?"

Hazrat replied, "The blessings of the Prophet (S) were bestowed on all the Companions (R). Some attained excellence in relating the hadith and some in writing commentaries on the Holy Qur'an. Even though the other Companions (R) also possessed knowledge of their inner selves, Hazrat 'Ali (R) attained excellence in this knowledge."

*

In Jodhpur, Mr. Badruddin asked, "Is it necessary to remain in contact with one's shaykh?"

Hazrat answered, "Spiritual progress that otherwise takes years of struggle is attained in a short time through the attention of a shaykh who possesses true mystical knowledge and has attained perfection in the vision of the Divine Essence."

*

In Madras, Mr. Nasiruddin asked Hazrat, "If you have something to offer, then why do you travel? People will come to you."

Hazrat answered, "It is a matter of time and expediency. The Prophet (S) himself sent deputations to other countries to convey the message of Islam. Hazrat Khwaja Mu'inuddin Chishti (r) and other saints came all the way to India. So, you can either travel to other places and teach or stay at home and teach."

*

In Calcutta, Mr. 'Ata Hussain said, "It is said that Sufi teachings expand human consciousness and increase spiritual insight and wisdom. I would be grateful if Hazrat would elaborate."

In response Hazrat said, "This can be understood through the following analogy. If you take a picture of yourself with a camera, you get an image of your clothes and external appearance. This picture will not show your internal organs. On the other hand, an x-ray or ultrasound will clearly show you how the organs are functioning. Ultrasound technology can provide information about the movement of the child inside the mother's womb. The reason is simply that the technology of the ultrasound is more powerful than that of a camera. Similarly, Sufi teachings lift the veils and illuminate the heart. This light allows one to see what lies within matter. This is why it is said that Sufi teachings expand consciousness and enable one to see and understand more than was previously possible."

*

In Dhulia, Malegaon, Sufi Sahib asked, "There appears to be a big difference between present-day saints and those of the past. Could you please elaborate on this?"

Hazrat replied, "The past saints reached their exalted status after a lot of hard work, perseverance and detailed knowledge of spiritual stations. It took them years of practice to perfect their inner knowledge and as a result the signs of their sainthood were evident. In these times, and especially in the Naqshbandi order, the seeker attains an overview of stations through divine attraction and transmissions from the shaykh, and seekers are perfected automatically without devoting extra time. Miracles are the products of spiritual practices and are not prerequisites for sainthood. The fact is, that as we move further and further away from the era of the Prophet (S) there is deterioration in the inner and outer spiritual dimensions. However, the inspiration of the present-day saints, especially Naqshbandi shaykhs, is not without Truth. The aim of the shaykh is for the seeker to become cognizant of the spiritual stations of the Sufi paths, not that they should equal the powers attained by the well-known saints of the past."

*

In Malegaon, Seth 'Usman said, "Some people have trouble accepting what Hazrat Shaykh Ahmad Faruqi Sirhindi (r) has written about his methods. I would be grateful if you could shed some light on this issue."

Hazrat replied, "Hazrat Shaykh Ahmad Faruqi Sirhindi (r) in one sense completed the Naqshbandiyya and in another created a new path which incorporates it. He wrote in great detail about the benefits and excellence of the new (Mujaddidi) teachings. Thousands of his blessed disciples (r) who attained the stations that he wrote about corroborated his claim about the knowledge and the states related to these stations. Their sheer number leaves no room for doubt. Other than this, intellectuals and scholars have concurred that the subtlety and the austerity of the Mujaddidi order is what makes it difficult for it to be accepted by some people. In the quest for greater spiritual development, the practices of the Mujaddidiyya lead to the development of faith and tranquility. On the achievement of one's goal, one experiences unparalleled exhilaration."

*

In Delhi, Maulana Badruddin asked, "What is the reason for the presence of elements within Sufism that are heretical and do not conform to the shari'a?"

Hazrat said, "There are three reasons for this. Firstly, once Muslim scholars became acquainted with the works of Aristotle, they drew excessively on logic and philosophy for theology. Islamic beliefs began to be reinterpreted through the lens of logic and rationality. This caused the doctrine to undergo some changes and opened the door to further innovations. Secondly, the influence of

Neo-Platonic mysticism led to things being identified as Absolute Reality. Thirdly, a pantheistic philosophy was accepted and this led, naturally, to less of a focus and finally a denial of the importance of the sunna of the Prophet (S). The criteria of sainthood changed; the ability to perform miracles, a by-product of the practices, was given prime importance. People began to think that spiritual ecstasy, the ability to have visions and perform miracles, were the real signs of sainthood. Unnecessary practices were introduced to develop these powers. The real purpose of Sufism – nearness to God – was forgotten in the pursuit of miracles, supra-human powers, and the desire to impress others by establishing one's superiority."

*

In Delhi, Mr. Rauz ur-Rahman said, "You have told us that one should have a goal in life. What do you think is the most excellent goal?"

Hazrat replied, "A goal can be big or small but the only true and exalted goal is seeking the nearness, the pleasure, and the acceptance of Allah. No seeker should, under any circumstances want less."

*

In Bangalore, Mr. 'Ali Nawaz asked, "The Holy Qur'an says that human beings are the vice-regents of Allah on earth. Does this mean every human being is a vice-regent?"

Hazrat responded with a verse from the Holy Qur'an (2:124), *My covenant does not include the wrong-doers.*

*

In Hyderabad, Mr. Muhammad Ahmad, who was very distressed, told Hazrat about his troubles and asked him to pray for him.

In reply, Hazrat quoted the following hadith: *Show forbearance when faced with the wicked intentions of those who are envious, for your forbearance will overcome them just like fire consumes parts of itself when it can find nothing else.*

*

In Tata Nagar, Mr. Mujib ur-Rahman asked, "Can spiritual training be given to non-Muslims?"

Hazrat replied, "If they are willing to recite the attestation of faith, it can be started. God willing, they will begin to receive the benefits. Compliance with other tenets of Islam, such as the ritual prayers, will gradually follow. According to Hazrat Imam Abu Hanifa (r), you become a Muslim once you have recited the attestation of faith, and the ability to do the practices can follow. When the non-Muslim Shyama Charan was given the transmission of fire, he had a vision in which he saw that a man made him mount a horse and took him towards a light.[3] The light was the light of Islam."

*

In Dhaka, Mr. 'Abdul Majid said, "I would like to read some books on Sufism. Which books would you recommend?"

Hazrat replied, "Some books describe events, while some deal with Sufi teachings. There are other books that contain essays on Sufism. The letters of Hazrat Shaykh Ahmad Faruqi Sirhindi (r) include all these genres. His writings are an encyclopedia of Islamic thought and Sufism. Also, if you find the opportunity, you should study the discourses of the saints."

*

In Calcutta, Sufi 'Usmani asked, "Why does religion need to be revived?"

Hazrat said, "When milk is poured from a clean and pure vessel into another one, and then transferred to other vessels one after the other, it is bound to retain some of the impurities of all the vessels that contained it. Eventually the clean white milk will become cloudy and impure. Just like this milk needs to be cleansed, religion needs to be renewed."

*

In Bangalore, Mr. 'Abdul Qadir asked, "What is the difference between the Holy Qur'an and the *hadith qudsi*?"[4]

Hazrat replied, "The Holy Qur'an claims to be a miracle, while this claim is not made for the *hadith qudsi*."

*

---

3. Fire is one of the subtle centers.
4. *Hadith qudsi* (a sacred *hadith*) is a non-Qur'anic saying transmitted by the Prophet (S) in which God speaks in the first person.

In Madras, Mr. Muhammad Hussain asked, "What is the difference between prayer and good etiquette?"

Hazrat replied, "That which is done out of fear of society is referred to as etiquette and that which is done out of awe of God is worship. Etiquette can turn into worship when inspired by the right intention."

*

In Purnia, Hajji 'Abdussattar asked, "How can we know God?"

Hazrat replied, "How can a blind person know what the sun looks like? He can either have surgery to restore his eyesight or he can be made aware of the effects of the sun. You feel warm when you sit in the sun just like when you spend time in the company of one whose heart has awakened. At the very least it awakens the desire for spirituality in you. Once the veils are lifted from the heart, a person is transformed. These things take time."

*

In Delhi, Mr. Ghazi'uddin asked, "Is there any difference in the effect if we refer to Allah as God?"

Hazrat said, "It is not possible to translate the word Allah because other languages do not have words which could convey its meaning. It cannot be translated literally. There are no words in any other language which capture the depth and breadth of its meaning. There is a big difference between the truth and falsehood. *La illaha illa Allah* has yet to be successfully translated in any language. Even if you do find a translation, it is fraught with controversy and disagreement. Since the attestation of faith must be recited in Arabic, it has been kept free of careless translations and spurious additions. Just as the meaning is unique and unknowable, so also the Divine Essence is beyond our comprehension. This is why the word could not be defined and has remained unknowable and undiscoverable. When the Divine Essence cannot be comprehended by the intellect and you cannot fully understand the Divine Essence, how can you define it? Yet God in His bounty told us His name and began His revelation with "In the name of Allah, universally merciful and singularly compassionate," and warned us to be wary of distortions of His word. Therefore a translation cannot compare with the original word. The Islamic concept of Allah cannot be found elsewhere."

*

In Orissa, Mr. Hardu Muhammad asked, "What is superior, the recitation of the blessings on the Prophet (S) and his family or the practice of remembrance of God?"

Hazrat replied, "If the student has learned to do remembrance of God from a shaykh, then in the beginning it is given preference. However, if the student does not have a shaykh it is better for him or her to recite the blessings on the Prophet (S) and his family."

*

In Hyderabad, Mr. Sardar 'Ali asked, "Are worldly fame and prosperity signs of spiritual excellence?"

Hazrat replied, "Worldly success and popularity are not proof of anyone's excellence, just as being accepted by creation is not proof of there being a Creator."

*

In Ahmadabad Mr. Jamaluddin asked, "Are the practices of the Qarniyya difficult to follow?"

Hazrat replied, "Hazrat Sayyid 'Abdul Bari Shah (r) used to avoid teaching the practices of the Qarniyya because in this path you are required to be in a state of ritual purity at all times. This is only possible for a hermit or recluse. In accordance with the sunna of the Prophet (S), our order requires us to live in the world and occupy ourselves with the remembrance of Allah. Therefore, it would be difficult for us to fulfill the requirements of the Qarniyya."[5]

*

In Dhulia, Sufi Kamaluddin asked, "The Holy Qur'an, the hadith, and the example of the Prophet (S) are enough [guidance] for a Muslim. What is the need for a shaykh?"

Hazrat replied, "The primary sources of guidance are the Holy Qur'an and the hadith. However, even between Allah and the Prophet (S) the angel Gabriel (s) was the intermediary. Now, if you want to learn an art, you can only learn it if you are taught by someone who has mastered it. In the same way, if you want to practice Sufism

5. The Qarniyya lineage is one that typically involves non-corporeal Uwaysi initiations and is named after Uways al-Qarani (d. ca. 657 Zabid, Yemen). Uways is said to have met the Prophet (S) in a visionary experience without ever having seen him in corporeal form.

you need to find a guide who will make it easier for you to follow this path. Ordinary Muslims do not need to pledge allegiance to a shaykh. Only those who wish to follow the Sufi way must find a shaykh to guide them and help them to proceed to the final destination without getting lost or wandering about aimlessly."

*

In Jaipur, Mr. Sharfuddin said, "There appears to be a weakness in the Sufi interpretation of Islam. Sufism seems to focus primarily on the Hereafter. What is the reason for this?"

Hazrat responded, "Even in the early period of Islam, there was a group of people who turned away from worldly affairs, as is evident in every period of Islamic history. This way of thinking was a result of their shortsightedness and narrow-mindedness, and had nothing to do with Islam. The Sufis remained apart from the government, but served as soldiers and advisors to kings, and prevented kingdoms from going astray. To consider the Sufis [of that era] simply as people of Allah and uninterested in worldly affairs is completely incorrect."

*

In Ajmer, Mr. Saulat Hussain asked, "What can one do to avoid being distracted by needless thoughts during prayer? How can one offer prayers in a state of being beautiful?"

Hazrat answered, "Ritual prayer is considered to have been completed when all the prescribed actions have been performed. Distracting thoughts do not invalidate prayer. The best way to attain to the state of acting beautifully is to spend time in the company of those who have reached that state. It is hoped that the effect of the association will enable the seeker to attain the state of acting in a beautiful manner. The best sources of guidance are the Qur'an, the hadith, and the lives of the Companions (R). After that are the experiences of the shaykhs. By following in the footsteps of the shaykhs, the seeker's path is made easier and the desired state of purification can be attained."

*

In Aligarh, Mr. Khalil ur-Rahman asked, "What are the benefits of doing the Mujaddidi practices?"

Hazrat said, "The benefits are innumerable. However, because the benefits are related to one's inner being they are not apparent to the non-initiate. In this day and age, people maintain that they are so caught up in the affairs of the world that it is difficult to take time out for practices. So, if someone sets some time aside from worldly occupation and devotes time to the remembrance of God, this in itself is a great achievement. Setting time aside on a daily basis leads to the attainment of certain spiritual states and strengthens one's relationship with God. This is of the greatest benefit. According to a hadith, the benefits of reciting blessings on the Prophet (S) and his family are such that whoever recites them once, Allah will multiply the blessings ten-fold. Reciting the blessings on the Prophet (S) and his family regularly will bring forth innumerable blessings and the effects of these blessings will also be felt in one's worldly affairs. Love is essential. Only the person who loves her profession can excel in it. It is also beneficial to have a mentor who excels in the profession that one has chosen. Similarly, sitting in the presence of the people of love creates more love for the Prophet (S) and Allah in the heart. This is how God-consciousness develops. Human beings are madly in love with the world. The goal of life is not the world. The real objective is the development of a consciousness that allows human beings to ascertain the true meaning of life. The goal should be establishing a relationship with God. If not this, then even the aspiration of becoming a good Muslim is to be considered a blessing."

*

In Medina, Mr. Abu Salih, a new disciple, asked, "What should we think during meditation so that we can attain concentration?"

Hazrat replied, "Our aim is not concentration but development. A yogi was once asked if the purpose of meditation was the achievement of concentration. The yogi fell into deep thought. After some time, he said, "My twenty years of ascetic practices were a waste!" In yoga you practice concentration, but in Sufism something happens by itself. There is nothing you have to do when you sit in meditation. For example, if someone sits in meditation, the blessings will begin to flow. Once the blessings come, the seeker is transformed. After one attains annihilation in God, one begins to experience different states, and drifts into another dimension. The effects manifest themselves. All the seeker has to do is make the intention. If the blessings are not felt due to insufficient light, the seeker will have to work harder. This depends on the seeker's capacity and ability. One has to turn away from one's worldly occupations and devote some time to the remembrance of Allah. The various sittings are meant to develop attention and knowledge of Allah. Due to the teaching, blessings will be received spontaneously. In meditation, nothing can be determined. If it is said that the seeker will see the sun, then it will not be the sun in Reality. All this happens in yoga. The spiritual realm transcends this world.

"Every seeker who perseveres can acquire understanding, although the degrees of understanding will be different. There are veils on the soul, and these veils can be understood as ignorance. The veils will be lifted from the soul once spiritual training begins and everything will become clear. There is the veil of interpretation, but otherwise only He exists. It used to require great perseverance and hard work for veils to be lifted. Now the path has been made easy, but it still takes time. Whatever comes will be the Truth, but what will come, only God knows."

*

In Pune, Maulvi Sirajuddin asked, "If our fate is pre-determined, what is the purpose of prayer?"

Hazrat replied, "Everyone is born with a certain destiny. However, this destiny has two aspects: the unchanging aspect and the conditional or contingent aspect. The unchanging aspect is written on the Preserved Tablet and cannot be altered.[6] However, the conditional aspect can be changed if certain conditions are met. Since we cannot know which aspect of destiny is at work we make an effort and pray in the hope that our misfortune is linked to the conditional aspect of destiny. When Prophet Abraham (s) was tossed into the fire, the angel Gabriel (s) appeared and asked, 'Why are you not praying to Allah?' Prophet Abraham (s) replied, 'Does God not see everything? One prays only if one thinks He does not know.' This shows Prophet Abraham (s) in a state of lordship.

"On the other hand, during the Battle of Badr, the Prophet (S), bowed his head in prostration and prayed for God's help all night even though he already knew how the battle would end. This state contains within it the exalted spiritual state of slavehood. Of the two states, the first appears to be superior but in reality, the second

---

6. *Luh-i mahfuz is* the 'Preserved Tablet' upon which the reality of all things was written before God manifested them in material existence.

state is more exalted. The latter, which contains in it an expression of helplessness, powerlessness, and humility, is considered more pleasing to Allah. The purpose of prayer should not be the alleviation of troubles or illness but the expression of one's powerlessness and helplessness in the presence of Allah. As this pleases God, we should keep praying to Him so He may be pleased with us.

Chapter Five
Nigarishat: The Writings of Hazrat Maulvi Muhammad Sa'id Khan

Sufism and the Modern Era

The modern era is about living life according to the dictates of science and technology, free of any kind of superstition. Every educated person is attracted to this worldview. Modernity is not about denying the truth. Unless a modern scientist is blinded by hostility and hatred, he must accept the invitation to the teachings of the Truth because even a single atom is not without value in his eyes. Nor can a scientist be dismissive about any school of thought aimed at the edification of human beings or any principle that leads to an understanding of the world around us. Scientific principles imply that human beings employ all the means at their disposal to establish the truth without prejudice. It encourages broad-mindedness and a tireless search for the truth, free from social dogmas and illusions. A scientist prefers to see people in search of reality, free from the chains of social dogmas and beyond the precincts of absurdities.

The purpose of education is to arrive at true knowledge and to inculcate sincere action on the basis of experience and observation. It is possible to receive such an education in a religious or a secular environment. The most important thing is that the education should be grounded in reality. A secular education focuses on developing the mind and strengthening judgment. Breaking through the inertia of thought and developing the rational and intellectual faculties is one of its highest goals. The refinement that this education leads to has its own attraction. But is it enough? Does refinement and intellectual development lead to contentment? Does it not leave room for any further quest? Does the conscience not cry out for something more? People can have pure sparkling water to quench their thirst, glittering air-conditioned buildings to live in, expensive clothes to wear, and jets in which to fly, but even the most affluent human beings continue to long for peace and contentment.

The enlightenment and the benefit education brings have led people to consider the mind the most precious part of their body. There is no denying the achievements of the intellect. Had people just led lives of ease and comfort, we would never have had the benefits of the marvelous inventions we see around us. With great courage and patience, people have used the power of the mind to turn the impossible into the possible. Detailed plans have been made for the exploration of the universe, but it does not seem to have occurred to scientists that human beings themselves, the creators of all these plans, may have within themselves other subtle centers of consciousness. If the universe around us is full of marvels, could there not be something miraculous about human beings themselves? Science has, unfortunately, limited itself to exploring the material world. If science had ever turned towards the spiritual world, it could have understood its realities. Scientists strive to benefit the world through their endeavors, and yet, had they explored the spiritual realm, they would have benefited the world immeasurably. Just like advancements in the fields of agriculture and architecture have provided comforts, in the same way, efforts made in the spiritual realm yield eternal peace, joy, and illumination.

Just as the mind is a center of physical consciousness in the human body, there is also a center for spiritual consciousness called the heart subtle center. People have gained significantly by developing the mind, and yet little effort has been made to develop this center of spiritual consciousness and thus the door to the spiritual realm has remained closed. Western intellectuals are not aware of the fruitfulness of this labor and probably think of those who undertake it as lost in superstition and illusion. If they were to experience this path they would benefit greatly from those who are traveling it. The need of the time is for the youth to turn away from useless arguments and debates. They must not be content to let wisdom live in books. They must embody it so they can quench the thirst of a restless world.

There is no denying that water quenches thirst, food nourishes, and fire burns. Yet if the relationship between cause and effect is disrupted, or the effect is opposite to the one expected, the mind cannot explain the phenomena. The heart subtle center, the center of spiritual consciousness, can.

The efforts being undertaken in this era undoubtedly have a future. We see people engaging daringly in new experiences. Others are so dazzled by the glory of the golden past that it has glued them to inaction and inertia and they wait for the future to unfold on its own. Knowledge of the heart as a center of consciousness is not new. History attests to the glorious record spirituality has had in the past. The question is why does the present and future appear to be so dark? The Truth must enlighten the present era.

O descendants of the keepers of secrets! Progeny of the travelers of spiritual worlds! Will you limit yourselves to venerating your ancestors? The descendants of Mill, Newton, and Darwin are not killing time by living in the past. The world is waiting for the successors of Ghazali, Razi, Rumi, and Mansur al-Hallaj (mart. 922 for saying "I am the Truth.") to challenge the materialists! It is waiting for the spiritual centers to show what is possible, or at least to show how the wisdom of the ancestors can be understood and applied. Atheism has not been happily accepted. It is born of despair. People want to understand and experience the Truth. Sufism is quintessentially about revelation and observation. Therefore, the Sufis need to guide the youth with great care and present them with models they can follow, so young people can free themselves from material concerns and can benefit from the holy world of light. Our ancestors were following the true path to achieve a great purpose. Although the descendants of the great royal dynasties like the Ghauris, Khiljis, and Mughals were forgotten, the doors to the gardens of knowledge cultivated by Qadiri, Chishti, Naqshbandi, and Mujaddidi schools of Sufism were never closed. The need of the time is before us and we are looking to the youth. Will the progeny of the enlightened not rise up? Until when will those who can reach out to the Hereafter remain trapped in the chains of materialism? I have great faith that my friends will rise up with great zeal and passion, and we will be able to develop a disciplined and coherent curriculum to reach the Truth. The illuminating light of the Most Beautiful Face of the Holy Prophet (S) will enlighten the souls who undertake this enterprise.

Invitation to Action

Praise and blessings on the gracious Prophet (*S*)
whose remembrance brings peace

The vigor and the stability of a community depend on discipline and organization. Weak discipline and lack of adherence to rules and principles can shake the very foundations of any community. May God protect us from such a predicament. It is essential to have breadth of vision, to be responsible, to look after the young and the aging, and enthusiastically and actively to walk on the path of Truth with sincerity and a willingness to sacrifice. One must think of understanding and speaking the truth as essential, act with responsibility at all times and in all situations, and wherever possible, avoid conflict. Every endeavor should be undertaken happily and cheerfully. One must be aware of one's surroundings and yet not be distracted from one's own work because in the end all human beings will reap the fruits of their own actions. One must make every effort to acquire the selflessness, the humility, and the ability for sacrifice that was characteristic of the saints. Above all, one must be concerned only with God and act only to please Him. This is the tradition of the saints.

In a community there are all kinds of people - young and old, good and bad, sincere and insincere. The important thing is to take steps without faltering or slipping back. Be warned that many have walked this path and were close to reaching the goal when misfortune struck and they were lost forever. Fortunate are those who can stay the course, inspired both by the hope and fear of reaching the goal. Once the goal is reached, every effort will be the source of good tidings and peace will reign. Take heed, this is the inheritance of the saints and must not be lost.

You are the successors of saintly ancestors; do not squander your inheritance. If you throw away the opportunity, it will never come back and you will live to regret it. Do not be led astray by the wiles of the devil. He has promised, "Except for a few, I will lead astray (his) entire progeny." He is full of wiles and eagerly looking for any opportunity to lead you astray. Your greatest success will be to be worthy of the blessings of God's promise as stated in the Holy Qur'an (17:65): *You have no authority over My servants.*

The Fruits of Effort

The benefits that come from effort are as clear as day. Success can only be attained through the alchemy of effort. Human beings are sensitive and have noble ambitions. There is a purpose to everything they do. They have good and evil within them. The result of an action will depend on the intention: if the intention is not noble and sincere, nothing good will come of it. Therefore, aligning the intention is essential:

> *If the first brick the mason places is crooked*
> *The entire wall will go awry*

Effort can be made for good or evil and the conflict between good and evil has existed since the beginning of time. In this world good and evil coexist. The doers of good and the doers of evil both propagate their beliefs and insist on the veracity of their claims. There has never been and never will be a place for evil in the realm of Reality.

When the specter of evil appears in this world, the righteous rise and obliterate it, and light is restored to the world. Goodness, like health, is a natural state for human beings. Evil, like disease, is only a temporary phenomenon. Ill health that comes as a result of mistakes or ignorance is not real; it is only an absence of health.

When there is a commitment to understanding the Truth, there is every possibility of attaining it. When the intention behind an action is good, the result is bound to be good. The true purpose of all action is to provide ease and comfort to people, to serve them, to protect them from oppression and violence, to rescue them from abject poverty, and to help them realize their potential and illuminate their heart with the light of Truth. Always remember, however, not to attribute success to human effort only. As a human being, where you have strengths you also have weaknesses, and hence are prone to making mistakes. This is why it is essential that you have a strong connection to God who has dominion over everything. People must take action, and in recognizing human limitations, they must carefully analyze cause and effect and understand that human achievements are His rewards. They must know that it is due to His blessings that actions bear fruit. If it were not for Him all hopes would turn to dust. Persistence, strength of will, and a contented heart are necessary to secure effort. Persistence is the very life of action. Without persistence there can be no action. This is why one must not be inattentive or neglectful under any circumstances. At the same time, no matter how much power one has, one must always be conscious of God who is the Bestower of power. This awareness is what makes us truly human.

Human Society

Human beings come into this world dependent on the bounties of nature. Without wind, without water, without the seasons, and without the animals and birds, we could never have survived. The need to relate and co-operate with other human beings is as essential to our survival as is nature. Therefore, the way in which human beings organize societies is of vital importance. The way in which societies can best be developed is through serving human beings and doing good deeds. This will lead to human beings becoming sensitive to others and true to their real nature.

It is important to determine what the real purpose of human life is, and we need to spend time deliberating which beliefs and way of life we should adopt. An in-depth reflection on life suggests the presence of a divine order. A relationship with God is of fundamental importance to the development of rules and laws that govern society. In addition to observing rules and regulations and fulfilling the duties and obligations enjoined by God, service and the respect for the norms of society are also important.

There are many forms of worship that have to do directly with the purification of the self. The question is whether the purification of the self is undertaken for creating an exemplary society or whether it is done for its own sake. The two are complementary. Purification and refinement of the self benefits society greatly as it leads to selfless behavior. In turn, serving humanity with detachment from other than God, with purity of intent and steadfastness, leads to the purification of the self. Whether it is a question of the purification of the self or that of undertaking any kind of action to benefit society, it should be done in the spirit of sincerity and selflessness. Life should not be idled away. What differentiates one human being from another is beauty of character not cast, creed, or color. Life after death is of fundamental importance to religion. Religion tells us that purification of the heart and the self leads to an inner knowledge. No matter how great one's achievement or how much people praise it, unless the hidden diseases of the self are cured everything goes to waste.

There is no denying that serving humanity is beneficial. At the same time, one must be careful not to blemish the purity of the self through one's thoughts and actions. Action is only a means which, when sincerely undertaken, leads to achievement. Neither secular nor religious people contest the importance of action. For one group, action is an end in and of itself, whereas for the other group, action is only a means to an end. Both are agreed that the result depends on the quality of the effort. For the sincere seeker, only results in the Hereafter are worth pursuing and the seeker cares little about temporary and impermanent results. The seeker is always vigilant because any unfortunate slip may lead to efforts going to waste.

Human beings should aim to reap the results of their efforts in the Hereafter because only these are abiding and real. One should observe the results of people's action as it is important to be aware of the actions and the fate of those who took the wrong path as well as the actions of those that lead to happiness. If people were to understand that everything in this world could teach us something and lead us to an inner knowledge, it would be a source of great inspiration.

In the name of religion, oppression has been sanctioned and unjust laws presented as religious laws. This has led people to reject religion completely and wage a war against it. They feel that while religion retains its hold on people they will neither prosper nor be humane. We need to consider whether this war against religion is a reactive movement or whether it has some solid basis. Those who use religion to justify the division of humanity into class, caste, and creed argue that the divisions in the natural world or in the human world are not a source of conflict. According to this group, divisions are natural and necessary to maintain harmony and order in the human world. Both this group and the group that rejects religion, value harmony and believe that the principles governing the natural world are important for maintaining peace and harmony within the human world.

However, we must understand that there is a fundamental difference between animals, plants, and human beings. The laws that are applicable to the natural world cannot, by analogy, be seen to hold true for human beings. The behavior of animals and plants is predetermined, while human beings have free will. Human beings strive all their lives to realize their potential and it is not correct to compare this essentially human struggle for development to the struggle for the survival of the species.

Different religions are not in conflict with each other, for they are linked to each other through a process of evolution. Religious people, due to inappropriate attitudes and beliefs often take a narrow-minded approach to the truth. Broad-mindedness demands that through observation and experimentation we expand our understanding so we can understand issues as they arise.

Laws of nature are different from the laws that govern human society. Laws that are flexible, suited to different circumstances, and made to promote the welfare of human beings are not the same as the laws of nature, nor can they be called laws of religion. When we talk about religion we mean the divine primordial law of the universe.[1] Since human beings have both strengths and weaknesses, and are liable to make mistakes in the search for Truth, the search for this primordial law is essential as a source of guidance. Divine law is an attribute of God that is manifested in the created world and is a source of progress and enlightenment for human beings, so no

1. *Din* is used in the Holy Qur'an in the singular and is usually translated as 'religion'. Although there are many religions, there is only one primordial contract between God and human beings.

society can oppose it. If people were to submit themselves to this law they would benefit immeasurably.

Are human beings free? Can they decide when they will be born and when they will die? Can they carry out all that they plan? Why is all this not possible? We have so little control over our lives. There can only be one answer: human beings are dependent on the mercy of an all powerful creator. It is due to God's beneficence that human beings receive bounties and the opportunities to realize their potential. If a human being willingly acknowledges a dependence on God and keeps the Hereafter in view, the person can perform great feats. The whole universe is dependent on the beneficence of God. It is the duty of human beings to know their limitations and be grateful to God.

The truth is the Truth. It can be known. To deny it is to deny Reality, and to turn away from Reality is to deprive one's self of blessings. This denial is tantamount to turning away from life and embracing death. It is to let darkness enter your heart. This is why the people of Truth consider those who deny it to be blind, deaf, and in a state of inertia. The result of inertia, indifference, and heedlessness is injustice. The deniers cannot see the truth, hear it, or act on it. The other disadvantage is that the treasures and secrets of knowledge to be found in the world of Reality are lost. These have the power to rejuvenate human beings. Those who serve the truth are transformed into noble and sincere human beings. Human beings have great potential, yet those who deny the truth can never realize it. The denial of Truth is no less than a curse. So look around you and let your decision be based on justice and truth.

Whose actions have borne fruit and who is suffering from heedlessness? Who has created the means of comfort for human beings? Who has plumbed the depths of the oceans and created submarines? Who has developed new technology for agriculture? Who has invented the radio and the x-ray? Who is responsible for new discoveries? Who has dominion over the air and space? Who established criteria for justice in governance? Who dispensed with violence and cruelty? Who did away with feudalism? Who brought about a revolution and broke the chains of slavery so that every human being was equal and free? Let the critics come forward and tell us.

Muslims have been left with nothing. Wherever you look you find only dust. Just as a voice can be recorded and heard after it no longer exists, actions can be known through their effects. Actions stir up nations and individuals. In the beginning the pace of action is slow, but persistence makes it gather force. After some time the effects become apparent. If the effects of previous actions were not to contribute to the effects of actions taken later, we would always find ourselves at the beginning. In summary, character and action carve out their own niche. Actions outlive the doer and their presence continues to be felt. This is why light is found in enlightened societies and darkness in ignorant societies. Actions have an abiding effect and continue to be a source of light for generations to come.

It is important to cultivate an attitude of humility towards God and bow down to him several times in the day so that the self does not become uncontrollable and work can be undertaken in the best manner possible. One should take care to eat clean, nourishing, and appropriate amounts of food as this creates an essential subtlety within the body that is a source of guidance. One should spend one's nights and days turning away from all that is other than God, seeking the pleasure of God.

Human beings are different in terms of their capacities. Some are more gifted than others. It is the duty of those who have more knowledge to believe that those who have less are entitled to a part of the knowledge that they possess. In the same way, those who have more power must protect the weak. This is how we can strengthen the spirit of service. Compassion and co-operation will lead to happiness and prosperity in society. To know this, we have to act upon it.

Invitation to Faith

Some people think that lawlessness and lack of harmony are the source of destruction in the world. They attempt to bring order by doing away with any kind of difference to be found among human beings, whether it is of caste, creed, color, or profession. These differences, they believe, should not be a source of privileging anyone or granting anyone special status. Just as nature does not discriminate in dispensing bounties, equality, brotherhood, and harmony should prevail among human beings. Differences must have developed due to certain circumstances, but they should not be considered permanent. The world is an arena for action. The capabilities and capacities of human beings should be the focus. Color, ethnicity, or lineage should not be a consideration. Nor should expediency be elevated to the status of religious law. No ethnic group should be singled out to be subservient or to rule. Neither should any profession be reserved for any particular ethnic group. These people want hard work to be valued and honored so that status is not a birthright. This way of thinking has, undoubtedly, led the way to achieving equality.

Now when we look towards Muslims we see a people in a state of decline. They are bound by tradition, given to rehearsing the glories of the past and powerless, without courage and the spirit of sacrifice. Wake up! Open your eyes and act! Your ancestors were known for their sincere and selfless efforts, their noble and exalted ambitions. Such were your ancestors, but who are you, idly waiting for a tomorrow that never comes? I have faith that you, the flag-bearers of Truth, will undertake great endeavors with zeal and commitment. After tasting the fruits of your achievements you will strive even harder and through your own enlightenment, you will illuminate the path for others. There is an ongoing war between materialism and spirituality. You must rise to the occasion. Let the realization of the time you have lost strengthen your commitment to act.

The materialists have illumined this world with their achievement, and the upholders of spirituality can also undoubtedly benefit from their efforts. For example, it is due to the efforts of the materialists that pilgrimages to sacred places can be made in a matter of hours! The materialists and the spiritualists need to work together to serve humanity. If they form a meaningful partnership they can become an indomitable force. Furthermore, if harmony can be established between the different schools of spiritual thought, then the world will ardently seek this rejuvenating spring of spiritual wisdom. Different religions are not in conflict with each other. They are linked to each other through a process of evolution. Religious people, due to inappropriate attitudes and beliefs, often take a narrow-minded approach to the Truth. Broad-mindedness demands that through observation and experimentation, we should expand our understanding so we can understand issues as they arise.

Broad-minded materialists and spiritualists have much in common. Both value freedom, compassion, and service; both consider oppression and slavery to be a curse; both view human beings as responsible and accountable for their actions. Even in the realm of economics both have similar views. However, for the spiritualists, the ultimate goal is the Hereafter while the materialists completely deny its existence. The belief in the oneness of God is the basis of belief in the Hereafter. The oneness of God can only be understood through someone who can explain it and make it manifest. If it could have been understood simply through the intellect, then the scientists and intellectuals of the West would have developed a deep understanding of it as they have great knowledge of the world around them. Experience and observation have shown, however, that where on the one hand understanding the oneness of God appears to be simple, on the other hand it is very difficult and takes a long time to grasp. If the true spirit of inquiry affects the materialists, then they will understand that there are no limits to research. What is unacceptable today may be acceptable tomorrow in the light of new research. Therefore, there is always hope that even if materialism reaches its height, the soul will still be restless for the truth that lies beyond the material world and it will soar to the illuminated world of spirituality.

There is a motive behind every action. The motivation could be selfishness and greed or it could be selflessness and service for the sake of service. Everyone prefers actions that are based on selflessness. The question is, how does one achieve this? Do we need to be guided by a wise and experienced human being to arrive at this knowledge or can we achieve this state by ourselves? There is a constant flow of blessings and bounties from the beneficent Creator but not everyone has the capacity to benefit from these directly. Therefore, the guidance of a teacher is necessary to achieve this goal.

If you are enslaved by your feelings and desires you will submit to them. Instead, if you submit to a Being whose commands have no trace of selfishness or narrow-mindedness, are full of compassion and lead to prosperity, then you will reach heights that lie beyond the imagination. It is a crime to turn away from the worship of such a Being. The only way in which a nation can protect itself from decline is by establishing a relationship with God, who is self-sufficient and all encompassing. The attributes that have been mentioned here are praiseworthy attributes. Is all this a figment of the imagination or is there really a Being with these attributes? A Being with these attributes must exist. The attribute of a shadow implies the existence of a Being with that attribute. When we see smoke or we hear about its existence from a truthful person we can be sure that fire exists. We know the Creator through creation. Logic leads the way, and the thirst for knowledge compels us to search for a Being who is merciful, beneficent, and has all the most beautiful attributes. We must endeavor to seek this Being. It is through nearness to God that we can inculcate virtues. Without achieving closeness to God we cannot serve creation or the Creator. Nor can we manifest the attributes of God.

The other fundamental principle is that of prophethood. Guidance can only come from a guide. The guide receives blessings from the Source of all blessings. Due to God's mercy, that prophethood is bestowed upon him so that he can selflessly serve and guide others, as directed by God, through revelations. Such a guide who is given a law is known as a messenger. The Prophet Muhammad (S) has told us that the Creator will destroy this universe and create it anew. It is essential to believe in this truth.

The duty of the spiritually aware people is to keep striving with all their energy and skill. They must strive to have enlightening experiences and observations, which will lead to success. There is no restriction of time and place because spiritual practices can be performed anywhere – in a mosque, in a Sufi lodge, in the desert, on the sea, at home, or during travel.

Our youth must also wake up from their slumber. As everyone has the same physical attributes, why then do some progress and others not? It is a shame to be known as an underdeveloped nation, therefore rise! Throw yourself into action and reclaim your lost glory. Enter every field of endeavor. Through your success show this acquisitive and materialistic world how gain is equitably divided among the people, how they should be cared for, and how one should fulfill one's duties towards humanity, one's nation and city. If there is little left after discharging one's responsibilities towards others, one should be content with it, because this is better than wealth hoarded by oppressing others. This is true contentment in the eyes of God. If a lazy and indolent man has little to eat and, despite his good health, refuses to earn his living, this is not contentment at all. Setting an example for others by earning one's own living and not being dependent on anyone is, in itself, a great service to humanity. This will help you to reach the noble goal.

There are two schools of thought. One is that it is important that people are valued and appreciated for their qualities and characteristics, and not the class and ethnic group they belong to. If the focus is on the person rather than the qualities, we become obsessed with class, color, and lineage, which make human beings prejudiced and narrow-minded. The other school of thought maintains that if the person is of no importance, then how can the attributes be of any value? Attributes point to the being they are associated with. If we get too entangled with attributes we will never arrive at knowledge of the being. The difference between these two schools is merely semantic. Both recognize the essential connection between attributes and being. The only significant difference is that one school gives priority to attributes, while the other gives priority to being.

An attribute has no existence if it does not belong to something that exists in and of itself. It would only be an illusion, just as a flower made out of paper has no perfume and the picture of a lion on a carpet inspires no fear. This focus on attributes has led to artificiality and the simulation of reality. Yet this simulation of reality has not proved useful when it comes to dealing with reality and facing it. The attributes and qualities that we see in this world are all contingent because the beings that they belong to are themselves impermanent. There is only one Being who has always existed and will always exist. He is not dependent on any one, He is One, He is all-powerful, the dominating one, the irresistible, the most merciful, the most compassionate. There is no weakness in His power. His domination is not dependent on having someone to dominate. His mercy is not dependent on having someone to show mercy to. His being a Creator is not dependent on creation. Even if nothing else were to exist, He would. All the beautiful attributes belong to Him. How purifying and intoxicating love of such a Being is, only the wise can know. How noble is the longing and yearning to be close to Him.

When we talk about 'being' we mean the permanent essence or particular identity that distinguishes one from the other. It is important to keep not only the attributes but also the person in mind, otherwise we will fall into error. It is only through keeping the person in mind that we can differentiate between the miraculous and magical. On the surface both appear to be spectacular but a miracle is a miracle and magic is nothing compared to it. One must consider the identity of a person before coming to any conclusions about that person's good qualities. That is why we must travel through the attributes to the Source. We cannot be content simply with attributes; we must know and have faith in the Source.

The Subtle Centers of Consciousness

The heart subtle center is the locus of guidance and theophany. It is associated with Prophet Adam (s) who is the epitome of humanity.

*

The spirit subtle center is the source of spirituality. It is associated with Prophet Abraham (s) who is exalted in friendship and the epitome of spirituality.

*

The secret subtle center is another center of consciousness, the glory of which is love, and it is identified with Prophet Moses (s) who is exalted in love and had the honor of speaking with God.

*

The hidden subtle center is a pure center of consciousness that is associated with Prophet Jesus (s) who is exalted in his splendor.

*

The most hidden subtle center is a subtle center of ultimate nearness associated with the Prophet Muhammad (S), who was blessed with the highest honor and the greatest nearness to Allah.

*

The self subtle center is the locus of discerning God's command (from the ego's command), the effect of which is to awaken one and bring about peacefulness and equanimity.

The Heart (*Qalb*)

The heart subtle center is a center of consciousness that is the locus of theophany. It is located two inches below the left breast. It can be imagined as a piece of flesh in the shape of a pinecone. It is both dynamic and sensitive. Its level of activation can be assessed in different states and in different ways. If the heart stops beating, a human being dies. If the heart is guided by its own nature or by the teachings rather than the norms of society and culture, then the entire human organism functions well.

There are two schools of thought. One is of the view that the human brain should be the focus of all efforts for reform; if the brain is activated and reformed, the entire human system will function well. Members of this group can be called the intellectuals. They take great pride in their intellectual prowess and think that their ability to understand reality is without parallel. They believe that guidance is not a gift from a Beneficent Creator but the fruit of one's own endeavors. They think that the structures and norms of civilization, culture, morality, and politics can be understood through observation and experience. For them the mind is the source of thought, emotions, memory, and perception. The five senses serve the mind, which has the power to create its own reality. It can magnify and inflate and it can minimize and deflate. It separates cause from effect, the part from the whole, and form from essence. It is the diviner of secrets and holds the treasuries of wisdom. Proofs of the power of the mind are easy to find. The miracles of technology surround us. The star-filled sky pales in comparison to the glitter of the cities. There is no denying the marvels created by the mind. Therefore, for this school, the mind alone is the center of consciousness and should be the focus of reform.

The other group comprises those who believe in religion. This school of thought believes the heart to be the center of consciousness. Although life courses through the entire body, sensitivity and consciousness, refinement and awakening, reform and purification have to do with the heart. They believe that if the heart is enlightened then everything within the microcosm and macrocosm becomes a source of guidance and joy, justice, and truth. Once the individual reforms, society is transformed; justice and equilibrium are established; and wisdom reigns supreme. Just like a minister with special status receives guidance from the Prime Minister, although many work under him or her and perform different functions, so is the heart that governs the human body. It would be absurd if the limbs were to declare their independence and rebel against the heart. The truth is that the heart is the most exalted center of consciousness. Those who have privileged the mind have made an injudicious decision because they do not know the secrets and ways of the heart. As a poet has said:

O Moses take a lesson from the intellectuals of the West
They have managed to cleave the ocean asunder,
But Mount Sinai they could not reach

Undoubtedly, the thinkers of the West have great achievements to their credit for they are responsible for astonishing material gains and technological advances. But the question is have they found peace of heart? Have they renounced greed, injustice, and cruelty? Has the lust for wealth and power diminished? Has their philosophy been able to help them to realize their full human potential?

When people become rebellious and disobey the ruler, anarchy prevails. They act as they please and unlawful acts are committed. A similar type of anarchy prevails within a human being when the commands of the heart are disobeyed. The heart is the uncontested monarch of the body. It is the heart that gives us the understanding that we need to establish a relationship with the Creator. In matters of consciousness, unlike the mind, the heart is not dependent; it does not need form to understand. It is able to understand both material things and subtle realties. It is able to hear the voices of angels and simultaneously exercise control over the organs of the body. Contentment comes to it from remembrance of God, awareness, and enlightenment. If the heart is troubled and disturbed, every organ is affected. Life not only becomes difficult, it becomes virtually impossible. Even the slightest sorrow is difficult to tolerate. Yet, if the heart is healthy, even great sorrow and misfortune will not do any lasting harm. On the other hand, if the brain does not work, one may not be able to do great things but life is still possible. When you embark on a journey, the hands prepare the map and the legs carry you to your destination, yet this is not a feat performed by the hands and legs themselves. It is the mind that directs them. Without it, the hands and legs could do nothing. Similarly, if the heart is not healthy and supportive, the mind cannot carry out its work. It is only when both the mind and heart work to their full potential that we can have the likes of the prophets Noah (s), Luqman (s), David (s) and Solomon (s) walk this earth again. The coming together of heart and mind will manifest itself through holy and valuable effects.

Some people may contest the value of the sacred in the modern world. They may think that what the world needs is effort and action in the material world. When needs can be fulfilled through effort and action, and human beings can be released from worry, why bother about the sacred which appears to have no utility? It is only when efforts are driven by pure and sacred intentions that human beings can truly live a joyful and prosperous life. We have innumerable examples from history of people who focused only on actions and achieved results without emphasizing purity and a sense of the sacred. History shows us how this has led to the world being destroyed over and over again. The confusion, injustice, and violence we find in the world are a result of privileging the mind and neglecting the heart. The heart has simply been thought of as an organ that regulates the body. The heart is the fountainhead of compassion, empathy, dedication, perseverance, gratitude, subtlety, and joy. Hear the voice of the heart for it is the locus of the light of God! It is the heart that has the power to immortalize and to create martyrs. If it had been left to the mind, it would have just produced a race of barristers and administrators. If it were not for the heart, we would not have objected to colonialism, nor would we have had the strength to rid ourselves of it without resorting to violence.

The mind belongs to the material realm and its inventions are so awe-inspiring that it has convinced people to live their lives according to scientific and technological principles. These are not the principles to live life by. For that you need joy, breadth of vision, empathy, equality, unity, humanity, and brotherhood. We need to create conditions for an open dialogue and ensure that opportunities for freedom of both creative expression and objectivity are there.

The teachings of reformers and spiritual guides are essentially about awakening the heart. In order to contain the lust for power, destruction, and the arms race we must see to it that the light of the heart continues to guide us.

The Spirit (*Ruh*)

The spirit subtle center is a subtle center of consciousness that is free of any impurity. When it is contained within the body, mobility, consciousness, emotions, and perceptions are created and nurtured within it. It is the command of God – the Divine command through which creation takes place. If a human being continues to receive the elixir of the spirit subtle center, it helps create an essence subtler than blood, which forms the etheric spirit that helps physical movement and working of the senses. This etheric soul is a part of human nature. No human being is devoid of its blessings. Believers and non-believers alike are equally indebted to it for undertaking action and performing tasks. The etheric soul evolves gradually. Food turns into blood, issuing forth in vaporous form until its movement can be felt in the veins. The etheric soul is itself subtler than matter, however its subtlety or density is affected by the kind of the food taken into the body. The more subtle and pure the etheric soul is, the further it can travel into the higher realms. The more gross the food, the harder its ascent becomes. The spirit subtle center can be further trained to better achieve its purpose through spiritual education, and through the influence of the other subtle centers of consciousness. If the subtle soul is nurtured with purity, good conduct, constant remembrance of God, understanding, and Truth, only then can it attain its full potential. However, if all the above attributes are present without the constant remembrance of God, a person can obtain some spiritual powers but cannot be a truly spiritual being. The seeker will only be able to achieve results in the physical realm through good outer behavior and subtlety.

Although the created world is a combined realm where matter dominates, due to the connection with the divine secrets and the world of angels, the light of the higher realms is also manifested within it. Only if faith is there to nurture this subtle center can a person become spiritual and travel through the various stations of the spiritual realm to achieve the fullest joy and spiritual happiness. That is why a person who has a subtle and pure soul is immortalized in people's hearts, even after the etheric spirit has left the body. The heavens and the earth grieve for the departure of a soul according to its spiritual status. When an impure soul leaves the body contaminated with filth and sins, that soul fills everyone with repugnance. It cannot transcend darkness and does not have the potential to fly to the higher realms. Imprisoned in the lower realms, it cries out for its own destruction.

The Secret (*Sirr*)

The secret subtle center is one of God's wonders. A human being is a microcosm. Every element in the universe is represented within this microcosm. At the same time, human beings have an identity that is their very own. They have an extraordinary capacity to gain every kind of knowledge and are the keepers of the divine trust and of divine secrets. Humans have, above all, the capacity to know the Truth. *We offered the trust to the heavens, the earth, and the mountains but they refused to bear it, and were afraid of it. But humans accepted it; they were ignorant wrongdoers.* (Qur'an 33:72)

Although every cell can perceive and feel, there are specific centers for different perceptions: the ears for hearing, the eyes for seeing, and the tongue for tasting. The mind, the heart, and the spirit also have functions other than bodily ones. In accordance with the capacity of these centers, God bestowed divine trust, showered blessings, sent guidance, imparted wisdom, taught human beings what they did not know and appointed an angel who brought His message. God made invisible realities visible and enabled human beings to perceive the truth of divine law. He endowed human beings with the inexhaustible capacity to contain the secrets of the universe. This is why humans are called keepers of the secret (sing: *sahib-i sirr*). The awakening of the secret subtle center leads to the revelation of secrets. When this center is enlightened, the person is filled with divine light, and secret upon secret is revealed. Once the secret subtle center is awakened, whether a person is awake or asleep, there is then an extraordinary level of awareness. It is through the secret subtle center that human beings receive spiritual intuitions and good tidings. This is why it has been said, "I gave my secret unto the mountain, but the mountain refused to take it."

The secret and heart subtle centers are intimately connected. The secret subtle center is really a part of the heart subtle center, and manifests some of the characteristics of heart subtle center. If this center is affected by heedlessness, then the capacity to hold divine secrets diminishes or completely disappears. The awakening of the secret subtle center greatly enhances the human capacity to know. The universe is teeming with secrets but the mystery of human consciousness has no parallel in creation.

The Hidden (*Khafi*)

There is another center of consciousness called the hidden subtle center. This center is about the silence that envelops secrets and keeps them hidden. When this center is enlightened, there are then no veils between the seeker and the unseen and yet the seeker does not lose self-control. That person has the fire of divine love burning inside, is tireless in striving, and, if confronted by death, still does not utter a single complaint. When the hidden subtle center is enlightened, the attributes of purity and God consciousness manifest themselves. Then a person becomes worthy of being called a human being. The hidden subtle center manifests itself in different colors in different contexts.

The Most Hidden (*Akhfa*)

The word most hidden (*akhfa*) comes from the word hidden (*khafi*). The control and secrecy associated with the hidden subtle center are intensified in most hidden subtle center. The most hidden subtle center overlaps in some ways with the hidden subtle center, but in certain aspects they are completely different. Human beings appear to be similar in attributes, such as hearing and seeing, but there is something unknowable which can make one human being so much nobler than another. When the most hidden subtle center is activated in a person, that person outwardly appears to be ordinary, but inwardly the seeker is joyously fulfilled on the path of Truth, vigilant at night, and as active as a lion in the day. The most hidden subtle center is a pure and elevated center of consciousness. Although all the subtle centers are essentially a part of the heart subtle center, if you undertake a detailed spiritual journey, then each one is different. Through practice and transmissions, a detailed spiritual knowledge is attained. Some people focus on the purification of the heart subtle center and do not undertake a detailed journey. Sufism has to do with the detailed spiritual journey. It is about performing good deeds, following the shari'a, knowing the details of the journey, and easing the difficulties of traveling from station to station with the guidance of a shaykh.

An example may help here. There are some general exercises that help us to stay healthy and there are also some special exercises for developing certain parts of the body. There are different exercises for the neck, the arms, and the legs. Although the objective of these exercises is good health, they also lead to the development of specific strengths. So it is those who focus on all the different aspects of the goal who have a much deeper awareness and understanding. This approach culminates in the subtle centers of the world of divine command reaching the station of what 'no eye has seen and no ear has heard.' However, the ultimate culmination is the purification of the heart and transformation into an exemplary human being who belongs to both the worlds of angels and creation. The teacher and guide on the spiritual journey keeps an eye on the six subtle centers and the four gross elements.[2] If the guide finds that they are stagnating, or in a state of heedlessness, he will awaken and enlighten them. He will use different transmissions to rectify the subtle centers and inculcate remembrance and contentment. He will take away the darkness and turn the subtle centers towards spirituality. These will become the seeds of perfection, and make the journey easier.

Some people think that the other subtle centers are simply stages of the heart subtle center's perfection and do not have a separate existence. Their practice and their journey are focused on the heart subtle center because they believe the purification of the heart leads to complete purification.

On the other hand, people who believe in a detailed spiritual journey say that the relationship between the heart subtle center and other subtle centers is like the relationship between the inner and outer aspects. Those who wish to gain detailed knowledge have to work separately on the subtle centers and on the four elements otherwise they can work directly on the heart and gain general knowledge. Through extinction and subsistence their hearts are immersed in God and that is where the work and the journey end.

---

2. The latter are four subtle centers of consciousness that have to do with the entire body and do not have specific locations. They are the four gross elements: air, fire, water and earth.

The Self (*Nafs*)

The self subtle center is an inner aspect of human nature that is not entirely subtle, for it is both subtle and material. It wants to assume the role of a dictator within the human body. It has a tendency towards rebellion, aggression, and hatred. If the self subtle center is not contained, it will vitiate the other subtle centers of consciousness and obscure their light. It can entrance human beings and distract them completely from the purpose of their existence, making them dance to its tune. When the self subtle center is not reined in, it tempts human beings into heedlessness and disobedience to God. Intoxicated with "only I exist and there is no one else," a person begins to think of himself as God. As a result, the capacity of the self subtle center to be steeped in obedience to God is destroyed.

Yet at the same time, it is possible for the commanding self to become the locus of God's compassion. It is possible for it to be nurtured by the compassionate and forgiving sustainer and it is possible for it to understand the reality of sin, to be ashamed of committing it, and to abstain from it. The self subtle center can let its subtlety blossom, using its powers to perfect and embellish physical and spiritual capacities. This propels a person onto a path that leads to the everlasting blessings of the Hereafter. If the spirit subtle center is responsible for creating movement within the body, the self subtle center is the source of will and determination. Each has its own properties and these must be kept in mind when we engage with them. The spirit subtle center embodies the divine command and belongs solely to the world of divine command. The self subtle center, on the other hand, belongs to both the world of creation and the world of command, forming a bridge between these two worlds.

Appendix A
The Letters of Hazrat Maulvi Muhammad Sa'id Khan

Hazrat encouraged his disciples to communicate with him through letters and received a fair amount of mail on a daily basis. In some ways a letter is like meeting. With letters, attention is exchanged between the addressed and addressee four times, and provides a source of transmission from the unseen for the person who writes the letter.

While attending to his mail, Hazrat read a portion of some of the letters and then keep them aside. Among the letters that he opened there were only a few of which he was able to read entirely. When I asked the reason for this, he explained that in some of them there is so much darkness that it is not possible to decipher even a single letter of the alphabet. He read these letters only after they had been with him for a period of two or three days. His response to the letters was very brief. The only words that he wrote were "*Al-hamdulillah* (God be praised), I am well. May Allah the Glorious provide ease." It occurred to me at one time that in order to simplify this process, this phrase could be printed and a blank space left for the name and address, but this never came about. If a letter contained an issue that needed to be resolved, Hazrat only replied to it after he had given the matter careful thought and consideration. Some letters Hazrat continued holding in his hands, even after he had finished reading them, from which it could be concluded that the writer had been favored with transmission during the reading and had received blessings and benefits.

On one occasion he asked me to respond to a couple of letters. In reply to one of them, while writing the phrase "May God the Glorious provide ease," I added the words "for you." Once he had read the letters and was about to sign them, he admonished me by saying, "Why have you added the words 'for you'?" scoring the words out with his pen. From this incident one is able to assess how many hidden meanings lay concealed in Hazrat's every word.

Some disciples did not write to Hazrat for months and only wrote when they had a problem they wanted Hazrat to solve. In the beginning of these letters they expressed their love and affection for him and then proceeded to their actual motive for writing. Aggrieved by their attitude, he said, "They profess such love for me and yet months pass before they inquire about me, and when they do, it is only to gratify their own need."

It was my practice to write one or two letters every week in the hope that while he was attending to his letters, one of mine would also come into his hands and I would be blessed with his attention. Hazrat immediately replied to the letters that contained some important issue or questions. Hazrat wrote longer letters to those who were in some capacity engaged in spreading the teachings of the order. In his letters to them, Hazrat wrote words of encouragement and discussed the importance of spreading the teachings of the order. One is able to discern Hazrat's deep commitment to the furthering of the order by reading these letters. His dearest wish was for people to commit themselves to this work with total sincerity and enthusiasm.

Hazrat took great care when he wrote to his shaykh, Hazrat Hamid Hasan 'Alawi (r), and beseeched him to pray for the smallest task, and particularly for the acceptance of the prayer for the furthering of the order.

*

Letter addressed to Pir Sahib (Hazrat Hamid Hasan 'Alawi [r])

Sayyidi wa Sanadi,

As-salamu 'alaykum. I went to Hazrat Sayyid 'Abdul Bari Shah's (r) Sufi lodge and to Tata Nagar. All is well and by the grace of God the number of people in the order is increasing. I received a letter from Rauz ur-Rahman from Delhi saying that there is a certain Azad Rasool who is eager to meet me. He might be able to come to Mathura on Sunday.

Including the holidays for Baqra Eid and Dasehra, the number of holidays will come to ten to fifteen days.[1] If possible I shall *insha' Allah* pay my respects at Ajmer Sharif. I met Zahur ul-Hasan in Calcutta. He is studying Arabic at the Masjid-i 'Aliya.
Seeking your prayers,

Yours truly,

Muhammad Sa'id Khan
September 27th, 1949

*

1. Baqra Eid is one of the names in India for what is generally known as Eid al-Adhha, when Muslims commemorate the ram sacrifice of Abraham (s) from 10-13 Dhu al-Hijja every year. Dasehra is the last day of a ten-day Hindu festival that celebrates the defeat of Ravana.

Letter addressed to Maulana ʻAbdussalam Sahib, Arkan

Respected Maulana ʻAbdussalam Sahib,

As-salamu ʻalaykum. Al-hamdulillah. I came to Chittagong last year as well. This year also, I have come on Hazrat's orders. Hazrat and all of us often think of you. We were glad to hear about you from Maulvi ʻAbdul Maʻbud Sahib last year, and this year we were pleased to hear about you from Mutiʻ ur-Rahman Sahib. You are aware of the deep interest that Hazrat Pir Sahib has in spreading the teachings of the order. Thank God that Hazrat is well and his health appears to be as good as it was when you last met him. May God grant Hazrat a long life and keep us always in his protection. Please tell us how you are? Hazrat is hopeful that you are doing your utmost to carry out the responsibility of spreading the order. We were happy to hear from Maulvi Mutiʻ ur-Rahman Sahib that the work of the order is progressing rapidly in Arkan due to all your combined efforts. The order is also spreading in India. Maulvi ʻAbdurra'uf Sahib is also working and this is how the order is beginning to spread in areas such as Bihar, Uttar Pradesh, Madhya Pradesh, Maharashtra, and Delhi.

Concerning Chittagong, Hazrat has instructed me to engage Maulvi ʻAbdul Maʻbud Sahib, Maulvi ʻAbdul Majid Sahib and Maulvi Fazl ur-Rahman Sahib for the work. They should be told to come and visit me at Azamgarh for a period of three months so that they may gain a comprehensive understanding of the requirements and responsibilities of spreading the teachings of the order.
Seeking your prayers,

Yours truly,

Muhammad Saʻid Khan
May 27th, 1951

*

Letter addressed to Maulvi Nazir Ahmad Sahib

Respected Maulana Nazir Ahmad Sahib,

As-salamu ʻalaykum. Al-hamdulillah, I am well. Although frail due to his age, Hazrat Pir Sahib is well. Hazrat's greatest happiness lies in the furthering of the order. He hopes that you will not neglect this responsibility and that your efforts will bear fruit. Please let us know how you are and tell us about your work. Hazrat Pir Sahib wants to know about you and he shall be extremely glad to hear that all of you are fully attending to your responsibilities.

We are pleased to hear Maulvi Muti' ur-Rahman Sahib tell us that you are working hard. We hope that the work continues to progress and that everyone works together. You are older and will undoubtedly act upon 'we are compassionate towards those who are younger'. The others need to respect and honor you so that they may be blessed with the attribute of 'we respect our elders.' As I was not able to meet you, may God give us the opportunity to meet. It shall be a pleasure to meet with you and learn about your work. Please let us know about all your efforts. It will be a source of great pleasure for Hazrat Pir Sahib. Seeking your prayers,

Yours truly,

Muhammad Sa'id Khan
May 27th, 1951

*

Letter addressed to Pir Sahib (Hazrat Hamid Hasan 'Alawi [r])

Sayyidi wa Sanadi,

As-salamu 'alaykum. By the grace of Hazrat's blessings Allah has given me the opportunity to perform Hajj. On the 23rd of August 1951 I received a letter from Calcutta that said a place has been secured, and if I wanted to go, I should immediately reach Calcutta. I was not able to meet with you because I had to reach Bombay on the 23rd. I was not very hopeful of arriving on time because Bombay seemed far away, but for the sake of the love Allah has for you, He made it possible for me to reach there on the 26th of August. I was informed that the ticket had already been bought [for me]. I also got a passport and have the good fortune to set sail on the 'Muhammadi' on the 29th of August 1951, the ship on which Shaykh Muhammad Sahib of Kohanda is also traveling.

Hazrat, I must entreat you to forgive any disrespect or impertinence I may have shown you because it is difficult for the likes of me to honor you as you should be honored. It is only your love that has permitted unworthy beings like us to take refuge in your holy presence. I beseech you Hazrat to pray that his servant may become a Hajji in the true sense of the word. May God forgive my sins and may He accept my hajj (amen). May He draw me nearer (amen).

May the darkness of sin and the veils of the ego be lifted. Allah bestows the grace of eternal light (amen). I need your prayers and special attention. Hazrat please bestow your special affinity on me and illumine me! May I be accepted by Allah for your sake. May Allah keep us ever in your shadow. May Allah bestow health and well-being on you and keep you safe from hardships and troubles. With grace, nothing is too difficult to accomplish.
Desiring forgiveness and in great need of your prayers,

Yours truly,

Muhammad Sa'id Khan
August 27th, 1951

*

Letter addressed to Maulana Muhammad Yusuf Sharqi Sahib

Respected Sir,

As-salamu 'alaykum. Al-hamdulillah, I am well. May God favor you with more enthusiasm and grace your love with good fortune and success. On completing the recitations on the Prophet (S) and his family that are recited after the evening prayer, continue sitting respectfully observing silence for a while out of love. Sufism is experiential in nature and one hopes to benefit from it. Instead of relying on one's own inclinations, the seeker should benefit from the experience and knowledge of Sufi masters. Retiring into the mosque in prayer to get away from the world is a kind of worship that requires one to disengage from worldly affairs, and dedicate time to directing attention towards Allah. Similarly in meditation, to focus attention on Allah, one has to remove oneself from worldly affairs and sit to the extent that one's temperament and capacity for love allows. What are the effects of this? When the seeker does spiritual practices, the effect is at times apparent to the student and at other times, one has to wait. It is not for the seeker to determine what the nature of the effect will be.

Withdrawing from external activities, observing silence while directing attention towards Allah, and if needed, engaging in some recitation and waiting for blessings is called meditation. This time is for the remembrance of Allah. Remembrance is at times reciting prayers and at others silently turning towards Allah. To expect anything is to block the flow and create your own constructs. Then there is the rush of thoughts and mental fragmentation, which ceases with the disappearance of impurities and darkness. It is like a spiritual person who comes to learn worldly knowledge, it is necessary to study various subjects and technical terms. Similarly, for your spiritual development, I think that you should follow the advice of whomever you consider to be the appropriate guide. One cannot hope to achieve anything much that is lasting through one's own opinions or the pages of a book. Each phase has its particular characteristics and requirements. Reading books has its own value. Therefore my advice is you mold yourself according to the counsel of your guide. An ordinary task may be performed on the basis of personal opinion. The guidance of a shaykh makes it easier to traverse the spiritual path.

Yours truly,

Muhammad Sa'id Khan
August 23rd, 1960

*

Letter addressed to Maulana Mukhlis ur-Rahman Sahib

My dear Rahman,

As-salamu 'alaykum. Al-hamdulillah, I am well. I received the letter that acquainted me with the situation. It makes me very happy to know that you all are striving to become enlightened and enlighten others. May Allah bless you with consistency (Amen). From the perspective of the Creator, if people fail to actualize their potential, then they have failed to perform their duty. When people who have the capacity to gain knowledge of the Divine and to attain nearness to Allah are content simply with the performance of good deeds, how will they fulfill the responsibilities of a higher office? The feats performed by the materialists in their quest for material prosperity are astonishing. They need to attend to their spiritual development. Simply eating and whiling away time is unbecoming for a human being. The path that ascends to the heavenly trees of *Sidra* and *Tuba*, the stages of drawing closer to the Divine Presence, have been traversed and described. To devote oneself to traversing this path should be the goal of the elect.

> *O bird that soars to the Heavens!*
> *Is it better to die than to accept the provision that hinders flight?*
> ('Allama Iqbal)

If Islamic centers do not encourage sublime aspirations, awe-inspiring courage, and nobility of character, then where will these be taught? People should hope for guidance from the Mosque of Guidance. There should be a place where people can quench their thirst for guidance, where those who are thirsty may, like ants and locusts, drink at a spring of sweet water. It would be lamentable if those who have been graced by God with wisdom and far sightedness do not put these gifts to use in seeking an inner knowledge. Being in communion with holy people is characteristic of noble souls. Heedlessness must be avoided in the centers for enlightenment. It is not customary for the noble to be satisfied with the trivial. Their way is to strive for the pleasure of God, to traverse the stations of nearness, and to gain acceptance. For this one has to keep in mind, "as long as the self remains, the path of life can never be smooth." One must pay attention to every breath so that not a single breath is wasted in heedlessness. There are some sacred moments in time, one should be careful not to deprive oneself of their grace. One has to firmly cling on to one's relationship with Allah because there is no room for despair as long as there is life. He values courage and bestows acceptance. People need to have sublime ideals. The straight path is open. The friends are striving. May Allah bestow His boundless blessings on us.

Yours truly,

Muhammad Sa'id Khan
May 6th, 1970

*

Letter addressed to Maulana Mukhlis ur-Rahman Sahib, Dacca

My dear Rahman,

As-salamu 'alaykum. Al-hamdulillah, I am well. I have received the enclosed letter and have become aware of the state of affairs. Efforts to attain constancy in results and practices are proof of a noble disposition and the felicity of the soul. May Allah firmly establish this virtuous quality so that the most effective manner of attaining the pleasure of Allah takes root within the self. Experiencing feelings of repentance without any cause augers well for a person's subsequent progress. It is hoped that Allah will soon bestow the gift of a tranquil self. In order to complete the infinite spiritual journey (*sayr wa-suluk*), it is not appropriate to stop at any place or station. Each dawn heralds a new beginning; every evening is a harbinger of felicity.

Committed people are consumed with a yearning, a passionate longing, and earnestly pray morning and evening, beseeching God for His bounty and entreating Him to protect them from evil. A moment of heedlessness, like a careless action performed with lack of awareness and regularity, becomes a source of anguish and destruction. It is said, "Those who procrastinated were destroyed." Everything in creation has its place. In carelessness there is the possibility of creating disorder. This is why punctuality and regularity are of the utmost importance for saints. May Allah bless you with the wisdom to value time. May He give you the strength to be punctual and regular. One's routine should be so established that one should imagine oneself completely confined by it. Not a moment should be free of action or spent in heedlessness. Rest and repose will come only after death. In this transient existence one has to strive for the eternal. Action and motion are intrinsic to life. If the pulse stops or becomes irregular, then life is endangered. Similarly, irregularity and lack of punctuality in practices can lead to confusion and chaos. As far as is possible, it is vital that practices are performed at the appointed time. Indolence and carelessness are to be avoided at all costs.

How disastrous the malady of indolence is for both individuals and society can be seen from those who have erred. Some lost their throne and crown, others lament their misfortune, and some have lost everything and become totally destitute. In places where there was joy and celebration people attained sainthood; where the fate of kings and dynasties was decided, nothing remains except regret and remorse. This unfortunate state of affairs is nothing but the consequence of inaction and breach of promise.

Committed and disciplined people should actively organize themselves into a group of companions eager to swiftly travel on the path. A group of people is needed who vie with one another in performing good deeds and achieving enlightenment and who will carry out the work with love and sincerity. May Allah save us from inaction and indolence and infuse us with a passion for action so we may be able to meet the needs of the time and fulfill our responsibility.

Yours truly,

Muhammad Sa'id Khan
May 13th, 1970

*

Letter addressed to Maulana Muhammad Yusuf Sharqi Sahib

Respected Sir,

As-salamu 'alaykum. Al-hamdulillah, I am well. In relation to the question of the 'I' and the 'heart,' it is apparent that the person who poses the question and person who responds, will be two distinct personalities if the inquirer believes in the existence of distinct personalities. It is evident that the difference between Zayd and 'Umar is due to their distinctive identities. Otherwise, in terms of their humanity, they are the same. For example, Zayd is distinguished through his individual identity. Now, Zayd's hands, feet, and different limbs and organs of the body will be under the command of his totality (the 'I'). It is possible that Zayd is stationary, but a part of him, his hand, is moving. Zayd, in his totality, is observing. In a similar manner, Zayd identifies the totality of his being with his 'I.' I am looking at my hand; it is moving. I am looking at my feet and they are still. To summarize, the sum total of one's being is identified with the 'I' and the constituent parts while the heart and such like are regarded as the limbs and organs. Where the reality is one unit then there can also be no difference between the questioner and the one who responds. There is only One. A person who recognizes that there is only One, should advance towards Reality and find the Truth. Getting lost in verbal interpretations, one is likely to remain far from the desired goal. God knows best.

Yours truly,

Muhammad Sa'id Khan
September 6th, 1972

*

Letter addressed to Azad Rasool

My dear Azad Sahib,

As-salamu 'alaykum. Al-hamdulillah, I am well. I am still recovering from my travels. Attending to one's work, and awaiting the bounties of Allah is the way of devotion. As long as there is life, the rebellion of the self will continue. May God's grace be with us in these trials. Every breath we take is like the breath of a soldier on a battlefield. A slight oversight and it's all over. At every moment and at all times one has to remain alert and aware of the enemy. God helps us to combat this enemy. It is not for determined seekers to get unnerved or despondent. High aspirations entail tests and trials. Consider people who are worldly. They spend all their lives experiencing profit and loss, yet there is not a complaint on their lips and not a trace of despondency in their hearts. Virtuous people should not lose heart or give up hope in this great and noble endeavor. This is the trick of the devil or the ruse of the ego. On the path, one has to flow along happily, that is all. One must not be discouraged by any circumstances. One must attend to and occupy oneself with the work. It is inappropriate, whatever the circumstance, to become excited or agitated. This is how a person is brought into the world. God's wisdom encompasses each and every aspect, which is often concealed from us. This is why it is incumbent upon us to hope for positive outcomes.

Destiny will take its course, so one should not become fearful and anxious. It is necessary to persevere with one's work. One should not allow one's thoughts to become a target for the devil. My advice to you is to remain consistent on the path and to follow the sunna. May God help you. Keep up the efforts to spread the teaching.

Yours truly,

Muhammad Sa'id Khan

*

Letter addressed to Azad Rasool

My dear Azad Sahib,

As-salamu 'alaykum. Al-hamdulillah, I am well. Received one of your letters yesterday and was acquainted with affairs. One should never proceed in an emotional and agitated state. May God fulfill the objective and may there be no difficulties. The matter does not only concern you, but along with you many others, and then, it has to do with important work. It is for human beings to strive and, by the grace of Allah, there will be success. May God help you and provide protection from the ego and Satan. The way of the virtuous is to thank God for His guidance and continue beseeching Him for future guidance. May God occupy us with His remembrance. Do not let this worry you. To be pleased with the will of Allah is to have achieved a high station. Allah does what He deems best. One should not fall prey to anxiety but resolutely immerse oneself in one's work. Confusion and perplexity are inappropriate. Live with gratitude and trust that the best shall come to pass because when Allah's servants wholeheartedly dedicate themselves to their work, the Creator assists them in their work and affairs. He is the One who accepts offerings. One should remember God with one's tongue and heart. It should permeate one's being.

Circumstances do not stay the same forever; to lose heart and to despair is not appropriate for those who love God. The vicissitudes and alteration of time and circumstance are only a manifestation of the bounty of the one unique Lord who is without want. He bestows on each individual what that person deserves. The covetous take pride only when something goes according to the wishes of their egos, but it is not becoming for the people of lofty aspirations, the people of the spirit, to feel aggrieved. There is no cause for anxiety.

Yours truly,

Muhammad Sa'id Khan

*

Letter addressed to Azad Rasool

My dear Azad Sahib,

As-salamu 'alaykum. Al-hamdulillah, I am well. Received a letter that acquainted me with the situation to some extent. On the path of realization, for those who strive, for the people of Truth, it is essential to hope for the best from God and live in the expectation of God's mercy and bounty. One must accept one's own flaws and mistakes, every time one stumbles. The Prophet (S), lord of the two worlds, may my life be sacrificed on his footprints, was at the highest station of divine love and acceptance and yet in the battle of Uhud against the Meccans he lost two of his blessed teeth. The extent of his prayer and vigil was such that there were cracks in his blessed feet. Although he had already been given good tidings *Such that Allah forgives your past and future sins, so that He completes His blessings upon you and guides you on the straight path* (Qur'an 48:2) he said, "Should I not become a slave who always gives thanks to Allah?" There can be no doubt that he was the beloved and the closest to God. Turning to any aspect of his blessed life is sufficient for our edification and guidance.

Hazrat Imam Husayn's (R) martyrdom, the poverty and the extreme hardships borne by the *ahl-i bayt,* the family of the Prophet

(S), and the difficulties that all the Companions (R) and loved ones had to bear, carry waves of hope to us in our stressful circumstances. Under these waves, the ocean is replete with treasures. The garden is redolent with spring and fragrant breezes. The diver who lacks courage may be disheartened and abandon his goal before it is attained. The flaw lies in the lack of vision, courage, and wisdom. A brave person neither turns and looks back before obtaining a rare pearl nor does that person let the tumult of the waves affect the pursuit. For such a person every defeat is an inspiration to move forward and only increases the ardor to overcome hurdles.

A servant of Allah, who is thankful for God's bounty and benevolence, considers his own efforts to attain the goal to be of no consequence. The person knows that God is just, a kind and magnanimous friend cognizant of every movement, every stillness, and every weakness. Through His loving kindness He provides opportunities for awakening the potentiality of His creatures. The surprising thing is that a servant who has such a master and who knows Him to be the cherisher and sustainer should, in the course of the training, experience frustration or despair – even fleetingly. For those who are selfish and do not have confidence in the benevolence of their Lord, say, "*If we had had a say in this affair then none of us would have been killed here* (Qur'an 3:154). God has addressed His beloved Muhammad (S) as follows, *It is not up to you. He may pardon them, or He may punish them. They are wrongdoers* (Qur'an 3:128). The people of sublime aspirations have praised effort, fervor, and enthusiasm. *A messenger from among yourselves has come who is concerned about your suffering and anxious over you. With the believers is he kind and merciful.* (Qur'an 9:128)

We need to devote ourselves wholeheartedly to practices that are in accordance with the sunna: *No person knows what joy is waiting for him as a reward for his [good] deeds.* (Qur'an 32:17)
Peace be upon you,

Yours truly,

Muhammad Sa'id Khan

*

Letter addressed to Azad Rasool

My dear Azad Sahib,

As-salamu 'alaykum. Al-hamdulillah, I am well. It seems as if difficulties have overwhelmed you. What you are doing is not right. If you have decided on something by yourself, you can certainly go ahead and do it, but the way of life that you are thinking of adopting in this world is merely a fanciful notion. Think carefully and do not act in haste. It is not right to rush into action when one is upset. Later, you shall understand better. From this distance it does not seem appropriate. If entanglement in worldly affairs results in less time for the work of religion and the desired results are not achieved in worldly affairs, how will you atone for the time that has been lost? One should act with courage and resolutely devote oneself to one's work. It is not wise to waste time on minor issues. Such a small group should not become so important as to make one neglectful. Love demands perseverance in work. Wait for the final decision and do not fear the future. God will help you. In any case, do not give so much importance to a small matter as there is no need to get entangled in circumstances. Let them pass. It is better if, like a patient person, you let time pass. May God keep hardships away from you. You must keep trying, for it is for the servant to keep striving. May God provide you with succor from the invisible realm. The teaching of the seekers should be appropriate and conducted with great care. May Allah accept your efforts. According to the divine law, one's true progeny are those to whom one provides spiritual guidance. One who is blessed with both physical and spiritual heirs is indeed fortunate.

Yours truly,

Muhammad Sa'id Khan

*

Letter addressed to Azad Rasool

My dear Azad Sahib,

As-salamu 'alaykum. Al-hamdulillah, my mother is also with me on the flight for Hajj. I have come to know of your suffering and grief. May God grant you patience. Suffering is an integral part of the human condition. It is best to accept Allah's will. A person is feeble. Everything is before the Lord and master of dominions. He is the supreme giver of commands. He has always existed and will always be. He is compassionate and merciful. He is the Lord of dominion.

A human being has to bow down before Him. In this attitude and nothing else, lies the perfection of a human being.

God willing, I hope to be able to travel to Ahmadabad this time. All of you must not grieve. Sometimes helplessness can become an obstacle on the path. Please excuse me this time. May Allah remove all obstacles and grant success and acceptance. Ardor combined with steadfastness is highly commendable. This is no time to despair. Carry on with your work. May God grant you ease and success because there is a lot of work involved in this undertaking. It requires more than courage. May God grant you courage and acceptance. Some courageous people are needed so that we may all unite and direct our thoughts towards a noble goal. May spirits remain high and God bestow favors from the unseen realm.

What could be better than if all our worldly desires were to merge into a single desire for Hereafter? May Allah make this possible for you. There is no reason to worry or lose heart because courage should draw inspiration from the bright future. We should not be affected by apprehension or idle emotion since in every act of the Almighty there is reason and wisdom. Make every effort to increase the number of the seekers of Truth. Our revered Pir Sahib is still weak. I have gone to Kohanda, and now plan to travel after the fourteenth. I am thinking of staying in Bandel for three or four days. Try to have more and more people join the order and a group of sincere seekers may develop.

Yours truly,

Muhammad Sa'id Khan

Appendix B
The Institute of Search for Truth Proposal

Introduction

Ours is the age of science and technology. The discoveries and inventions of science have placed material resources in the control of human beings and humanity is continually striving to exploit the Earth's natural resources to achieve its own ends. Science has endowed human beings with such a capacity to understand and master the universe, that today they aspire to travel to Mars and beyond. In spite of these advances, however, it is undeniable that human life on the whole is still devoid of peace and tranquility. The human being of today may be compared to a child who enters a huge and magnificent factory; because of an inquisitive and restless nature, the person sets the machinery in motion and then is puzzled and bewildered. This person looks on helplessly as it runs out of control and is at a loss to understand how to control the power and energy generated by the machinery and make beneficial use of it. The person's mind is overwhelmed with the apprehension that this gigantic factory of machinery may crush and destroy everything.

The Modern Person's Error

The fundamental error of the modern human being has been the continuous focus on external reality, making it the exclusive object of his study and research, utterly neglectful of that world which lies hidden within. The modern human being has attached very little importance to the inner self and to inner powers. Science depends on observation, experience, and logic, but it is short sighted to believe that human powers are confined only to a few sense perceptions or a few powers of thinking and reasoning. Scientists have not made any significant attempts to find out about other aspects of human existence because they are unaware of their own selves and potentialities. Consequently, their knowledge of the external world is incomplete and moreover, they are ignorant of the principles and rules for the proper utilization of this knowledge for human benefit. Most Western thinkers who care about humanity and have a scientific perspective, gradually come to realize that science/technology, with all its advancement, has failed to find the remedy for human suffering.

Science/technology has often added to the problems confronting human beings. Today, philosophers, politicians, scientists, and social reformers are striving to alleviate human suffering, but they are no closer to the desired goal. Science itself has brought humanity to a stage where it is faced with a dilemma. It cannot abandon the scientific approach. Yet, scientific achievements and discoveries not only do not satisfy humanity, but advances in science and the scientific method, with its concentration on a materialistic and self-centered approach, have plunged humanity into chaos and placed it on a path of self-destruction. The materialistic approach divides humankind and sows the seed of mutual hatred and selfishness, leading to conflict and clashes between different interests and classes, and between the planet itself and its inhabitants - inhabitants who are supposed to be its stewards.

The Remedy

The only way out is to conceptualize the scientific approach and experimental methods in a wider perspective and use them for investigating a path which extricates humanity from its suffering, bringing it into a state of peace and equilibrium. It is obvious that the remedy for the ills of humanity is to be found in human nature itself. The study of external reality alone cannot yield the true knowledge for the fulfillment of human nature. A deep study of human nature and an exploration and investigation of the inner world of human beings will acquaint us with the true destination of man and the means for reaching it. The different creeds of religion and spirituality are nothing but elaborations of this fundamental truth. However, these elaborations are based on the spiritual experiences of the different founders of religions and moral reformers.

The Institute

The Institute of Search for Truth is founded on these observations and insights. The Institute is based on the firm conviction that as atoms have unlimited potentialities and powers hidden within them, the most evolved form of matter - the human body - is bound to be a reservoir of greater powers and wonders. To search out this wonderful treasure is the aim of our Institute. The existence of a human being's inner powers is not a figment of the imagination. Modern psychology, particularly the psychology of the unconscious, points to such vistas of human nature which can reveal many hidden facts and secrets of the human self. By way of illustration, we may refer to the discoveries of C.G. Jung who in his investigations uncovered aspects of human nature that brought his psychology very close to mysticism. His work paved the way for the modern investigators of the mind and brain such as Robert Ornstein and Arthur Deikman.

Aims and Objectives

In brief, we can state the purpose of the Institute as follows:
The aim of the Institute is to investigate those areas of human nature and the hidden sources of human knowledge that have not yet been explored by science and reason. This investigation has to follow a modern and refined scientific approach and experiential method. In this way, finding the solutions to various human problems and the remedy for different human ills will be undertaken. The Institute strives to understand the essential nature of humans, the universe, and humanity's relation to it in a way relevant to the contemporary world.

This understanding will help us to find solutions to the problems of the individual and collective life of humanity. While material energy and discoveries can and should be utilized in the service of humanity, the main objective of the Institute is to discover the capabilities and potentialities of the inner human being, and their utilization for the benefit of humankind.

The hidden power of the human self, which we are seeking to tap and utilize, is the power of love. It is this power that frees human beings from the bonds of narrow materialism and selfishness, and persuades them to observe tolerance, sympathetic regard, benevolence, and self-sacrifice towards others. It motivates, inspires, challenges, and satisfies. The understanding of the nature of the self and its hidden powers will be conducive to adjusting our attitudes and behavior to others and to the universe as a whole. It will reveal to us the powerful inter-relatedness of the human existence and the universe, and will bring forth a creed of universal brotherhood and unbounded love.

The Policy

The policy and creed of our Institute is synonymous with the creed of "peace with all." Any conflict with any religion or creed is totally excluded from our aims and policy, but it is obvious that for the implementation of its objectives, the Institute will recommend a specific program of practical exercises. Though this program will not be in conflict with those of other creeds or institutes, it will follow specific lines of its own and will exhibit a few special features that we have learned from those who have guided us and traveled on this Path.

The Technique

To awaken the hidden powers of the self and make them operative in life, the technique of the Institute consists of a special form of meditation. This meditation results in an intuitive insight that enables us to begin to see all things in their true perspective, and to understand the truths about life and the universe in a proper light. It further opens up a new way of thinking that gives life a correct direction, develops one's character, and provides a healthy ideal. It creates enough sincerity of purpose to correct the distorted notions and misguided actions of our life. In short, it serves to build up a noble personality and to discipline and optimize our lives.

Everyone who values an empirically-based approach to inquiry, has a genuine yearning for knowledge, and wishes to understand the reality of life is invited to try our techniques. An individual's adherence to any philosophical creed or religion is not important in this process. It is suggested that any person who is interested in our work should come and stay with us for at least one week, observe, and test our techniques. Only after close observation and through practical experience will a person be in a position to assess the true value of our work. However, those persons who are, at the moment, unable to undertake the journey to Delhi and stay at our Institute, can acquaint themselves with our techniques through correspondence. We shall send them instructions for their guidance.This outline is meant to give our readers some idea about the Institute. The Institute does not aim at propounding or rationally explaining philosophical problems or theoretical creeds. It simply seeks to promote a Path purely of experience and actual practice. For necessary information, instructions, and enquiries please write to the Director of the Institute.

Azad Rasool
1975

Appendix C
Shajarat i-Tayyiba (Lineages) of the Mujaddidī, Naqshbandī, Qādirī, Chishtī, and Shādhilī Orders

Appendix D
Shajarat i-Tayyiba (Lineages) with Sufi Masters' Dates and Locations

The Prophet

The Caliph Abū Bakr aṣ-Ṣiddīq ﷺ

Naqshbandī Silsila

Ḥaḍrat Salmān Fārsī ﷺ
Ḥaḍrat Qāsim ibn Muḥammad ibn Abī Bakr (r)
Ḥaḍrat Imām Jā'far aṣ-Ṣādiq (r)
Ḥaḍrat Shaykh Abū Yazīd Tayfūr Bisṭāmī (r)
Ḥaḍrat Abū'l-Ḥasan 'Alī ibn Aḥmad Kharaqānī (r)
Ḥaḍrat Abū'Alī Fārmadī Ṭūsī (r)
Ḥaḍrat Abū Ya'qūb Yūsuf Hamadānī (r)
Ḥaḍrat Khwājah 'Abd al-Khāliq Ghujduwānī (r)
Ḥaḍrat Mawlānā 'Ārif Rīwgarī (r)
Ḥaḍrat Khwājah Maḥmūd Abū al-Khayr Anjīr Faghnawī (r)
Ḥaḍrat 'Azīzān 'Alī Rāmitanī (r)
Ḥaḍrat Mawlānā Muḥammad Bābā Sammāsī (r)
Ḥaḍrat Sayyid Amīr Kulāl (r)
Ḥaḍrat Khwājah Muḥammad Bahā'uddīn Shāh Naqshband (r)

Ḥaḍrat Khwājah 'Alā'uddīn al-'Aṭṭār (r)
Ḥaḍrat Mawlānā Ya'qūb Charkhī (r)
Ḥaḍrat Khwājah 'Ubaydullāh Aḥrār (r)
Ḥaḍrat Mawlānā Muḥammad az-Zāhid Wakhshī (r)
Ḥaḍrat Mawlānā Darwīsh Muḥammad (r)
Ḥaḍrat Mawlānā Muḥammad Khwājah Amkanagī (r)
Ḥaḍrat Khwājah Muḥammad Bāqībillāh (r)
Ḥaḍrat Imām Rabbānī Shaykh Aḥmad Farūqī Sirhindī (r)

Mujaddidī Silsila

Ḥaḍrat Ādam Banūrī (r)
Ḥaḍrat Sayyid 'Abdullāh Akbarābādī (r)
Ḥaḍrat Shāh 'Abd ar-Raḥīm (r)
Ḥaḍrat Shāh Walīullāh (r)
Ḥaḍrat Shāh 'Abd al-'Azīz (r)
Ḥaḍrat Sayyid Aḥmad Shahīd (r)
Ḥaḍrat Ṣūfī Nūr Muḥammad (r)
Ḥaḍrat Ṣūfī Fātiḥ 'Alī Uwaysī (r)
Ḥaḍrat Mawlānā Ghulām Salmānī (r)

Shādhilī Silsila

Ḥaḍrat Imām Ḥusayn ﷺ
Ḥaḍrat Shaykh Muḥammad Jārbadī (r)
Ḥaḍrat Shaykh Sa'īd Qīrwānī (r)
Ḥaḍrat Shaykh Fatiḥ Mas'ūdī (r)
Ḥaḍrat Shaykh Abū al-Qāsim Mīrwānī (r)
Ḥaḍrat Shaykh Abū Is'ḥāq Ibrāhīm Baṣrī (r)
Ḥaḍrat Shaykh Quṭbuddīn Mahmūd Qazwīnī (r)
Ḥaḍrat Shaykh Shamsuddīn (r)
Ḥaḍrat Shaykh Tājuddīn (r)
Ḥaḍrat Shaykh Abū al-Ḥasan 'Alī (r)
Ḥaḍrat Shaykh Taqīuddīn Ṣūfī (r)
Ḥaḍrat Shaykh Sharafuddīn Madanī (r)
Ḥaḍrat Shaykh 'Abd as-Salām ibn Mashīsh (r)
Ḥaḍrat Shaykh Nūruddīn Abū al-Ḥasan Shādhilī (r)

Muḥammad ﷺ

The Caliph Ḥaḍrat ʿAlī ibn Abī Ṭālib ؓ

Chishtī Silsila

Ḥaḍrat Ḥasan Baṣrī (r)
Ḥaḍrat Abū al-Faḍl ʿAbd al- Wāḥid ibn Zayd (r)
Ḥaḍrat Abū al-Fayḍ Fuḍayl ibn ʿIyāḍ (r)
Ḥaḍrat Ibrāhīm ibn Adham Balkhī (r)
Ḥaḍrat Khwājah Sadīduddīn Ḥudhayfah Marʿashī (r)
Ḥaḍrat Khwājah Amīnuddīn Abū Hubayrah Baṣrī (r)
Ḥaḍrat Khwājah Mamshād ʿUlw Dīnawarī (r)
Ḥaḍrat Khwājah Abū Isʾḥāq Shāmī Chishtī (r)
Ḥaḍrat Khwājah Abū Aḥmad ibn Farasnafa (r)
Ḥaḍrat Khwājah Abū Muḥammad ibn Aḥmad (r)
Ḥaḍrat Khwājah Abū Yūsuf Chishtī (r)
Ḥaḍrat Muḥammad Mawdūd Chishtī (r)
Ḥaḍrat Ḥajjī Sharīf Zindānī (r)
Ḥaḍrat Khwājah ʿUthmān Harvanī (r)
Ḥaḍrat Khwājah Muʿīnuddīn Chishtī (r)
Ḥaḍrat Quṭbuddīn Bakhtiyār Kākī (r)
Ḥaḍrat Farīduddīn Masʿūd Ganj-i Shakar (r)
Ḥaḍrat Khwājah Niẓāmuddīn Awliyāʾ (r)
Ḥaḍrat Naṣīruddīn Chirāgh-i Delhī (r)
Ḥaḍrat Kamāluddīn ʿAllāma (r)
Ḥaḍrat Sirājuddīn (r)
Ḥaḍrat ʿIlmuddīn (r)
Ḥaḍrat Maḥmūd (r)
Ḥaḍrat Jamāluddīn (r)
Ḥaḍrat Ḥasan (r)
Ḥaḍrat Muḥammad (r)
Ḥaḍrat Muḥammad Yaḥyā Madanī (r)
Ḥaḍrat Mawlānā Kalīmullāh Jahānābādī (r)
Ḥaḍrat Mawlānā Niẓāmuddīn (r)
Ḥaḍrat Mawlānā Fakhruddīn (r)
Ḥaḍrat Mawlānā Shāh Niyāz Aḥmad (r)
Ḥaḍrat Mawlānā Shaykh Miskīn (r)
Ḥaḍrat Mawlānā Nijābat ʿAlī Shāh (r)
Ḥaḍrat Abū Ḥāmid Karīm Bakhsh (r)

Ḥaḍrat Sayyid ʿAbd al-Bāri Shāh (r)
Ḥaḍrat Ḥāfiẓ Ḥāmid Ḥasan ʿAlawī (r)
Ḥaḍrat Muḥammad Saʿīd Khān (r)
Ḥaḍrat Azad Rasool (r)
Ḥaḍrat Ḥāmid Ḥasan

Qādirī Silsila

Ḥaḍrat Imām Ḥusayn ؓ
Ḥaḍrat Imām ʿAlī Zayn al-ʿĀbidīn (r)
Ḥaḍrat Imām Muḥammad Bāqir (r)
Ḥaḍrat Imām Jāʿfar aṣ-Ṣādiq (r)
Ḥaḍrat Imām Mūsā al-Kāẓim (r)
Ḥaḍrat Imām Mūsā Riḍā (r)
Ḥaḍrat Maʿrūf Karkhī (r)
Ḥaḍrat Sarī Saqaṭī (r)
Ḥaḍrat Junayd Baghdādī (r)
Ḥaḍrat Shaykh Abū Bakr Shiblī (r)
Ḥaḍrat Shaykh ʿAbd al-ʿAzīz Tamīmī (r)
Ḥaḍrat Abū al-Faḍl Abū al-Wāḥid Tamīmī (r)
Ḥaḍrat Abū al-Faraḥ Tarṭūsī (r)
Ḥaḍrat Abu al-Ḥasan Farshī (r)
Ḥaḍrat Abū Saʿīd al-Mubārak Mukharrimī (r)
Ḥaḍrat Shaykh ʿAbd al-Qādir Jīlānī (r)

The appendices document the lines of teachers through whom the author's predecessors traced their spiritual descent from the Prophet Muhammad ﷺ. For clarity's sake, the numerous parallel branches that have extended from shaykhs with multiple khalifahs (deputies) are not shown.

——— Direct connection

.... *uwaysi* connection (by internal transmission)

Naqshbandī-Mujaddidī	Dates	Place Born and/or Lived	Place Died
The Prophet Muḥammad ﷺ	570-632 (51 B.H. - 10 A.H.)	Mecca, Medina	Medina
The Caliph Abū Bakr aṣ-Ṣiddīq ؓ	571-634 (50 B.H. - 13 A.H.)	Mecca, Medina	Medina
Salmān Fārisī ؓ	d. 655 (356)	Isfahan (Persia), Syria, Medina, Ctesiphon (Persia)	Jerusalem
Ḥaḍrat Qāsim ibn Muḥammad ibn Abī Bakr (r)	655-726 (37-108)	Medina	Qudayd (near Medina)
Ḥaḍrat Imām Jā'far aṣ-Ṣādiq (r)	702-765 (83-148)	Medina	Medina
Ḥaḍrat Shaykh Abū Yazīd Tayfūr Bisṭāmī (r)	d. 875 (261)	Syria, Persia	Damascus or Bistam (Persia)
Ḥaḍrat Abū al-Ḥasan 'Alī ibn Aḥmad Kharaqānī (r)	953 or 962/64–1033 (341 or 350/52-425)	Kharaqan (near Bistam, in Khurasan, Persia)	Kharaqan
Ḥaḍrat Abū 'Alī al-Fārmadī Ṭūsī (r)	d. 1084 (477)	Khurasan (Persia)	Farmad (near Tus, Persia)
Ḥaḍrat Abū Ya'qūb Yūsuf al-Hamadānī (r)	1048-1140 (440-535)	Buzanjird (near Hamadan, Persia), Baghdad, Isfahan, Bukhara (Central Asia)	Merv (Persia)
Ḥaḍrat Khwājah 'Abd al-Khāliq Ghujduwānī (r)	d. 1179 (575) or 1220 (617)	Ghujduwān (near Bukhara), Bukhara	
Ḥaḍrat Mawlānā 'Ārif Rīwgarī (r)	d. 1219 (616) or 1239 (636)	Bukhara	Riwakar (near Bukhara)
Ḥaḍrat Khwājah Mahmūd Abū al-Khayr Anjīr Faghnawī (r)	d. 1245 (643) or 1272 (670) or 1317 (717)	Bukhara	Qilit (near Bukhara)
Ḥaḍrat 'Azīzān 'Alī Rāmitanī (r)	d. 1239 (636) or 1315 (715) or 1321 (721)	Bukhara	Khwarazm (Central Asia)
Ḥaḍrat Mawlānā Muḥammad Bābā Sammāsī (r)	d. 1340 (740) or 1354 (755)	Bukhara	Samas (near Bukhara)
Ḥaḍrat Sayyid Amīr Kulāl (r)	d. 1370 (772)	Bukhara	Sukhar (near Bukhara)
Ḥaḍrat Khwājah Muḥammad Bahā'uddīn Shāh Naqshband (r)	1317-1389 (717-791)	Bukhara	Bukhara
Ḥaḍrat Khwājah 'Alā'uddīn al-'Aṭṭār (r)	d. 1400 (803)	Khwarazm (Central Asia)	Jaganyan (near Bukhara)
Ḥaḍrat Mawlānā Ya'qūb al-Charkhī (r)	d. 1447 (851)	Charkh (Afghanistan), Central Asia	Hisar (near Dushanbe, Tajikistan)
Ḥaḍrat Khwājah 'Ubaydullāh Aḥrār (r)	1404-1490 (804-896)	Tashkent (Central Asia)	Kaman Kashan near Samarqand
Ḥaḍrat Mawlānā Muḥammad az-Zāhid Wakhshī (r)	d. 1529 (936)	Central Asia	Samarqand
Ḥaḍrat Mawlānā Darwīsh Muḥammad (r)	d. 1562 (970)	Central Asia	Samarqand
Ḥaḍrat Mawlānā Muḥammad Khwājah al-Amkanagī (r)	d. 1600 (1008)	Bukhara	Shash (Afghanistan)
Ḥaḍrat Khwājah Muḥammad Bāqībillāh (r)	1564-1603 (972-1012)	Kabul, Delhi	Delhi
Ḥaḍrat Imām Rabbānī Shaykh Aḥmad Fārūqī Sirhindī (r)	564-1625 (972-1034)	Sirhind (India)	Sirhind

Ḥaḍrat Ādam Banūrī (r)	d. 1643 (1053)		Medina
Ḥaḍrat Sayyid ‘Abdullāh Akbarābādī (r)			Agra (India)
Ḥaḍrat Shāh ‘Abd ar-Raḥīm (r)	d. 1719 (1131/32)	Delhi	Delhi
Ḥaḍrat Shāh Walīullāh (r)	1702-1762 (1114-1176)	Delhi, Medina	Delhi
Ḥaḍrat Shāh ‘Abd al-‘Azīz (r)	1746-1824 (1159-1239)	Delhi	Delhi
Ḥaḍrat Sayyid Aḥmad Shahīd (r)	1786-1831 (1201-1246)	Bareilly (India), Delhi	Balakot (India)
Ḥaḍrat Ṣūfī Nūr Muḥammad (r)			Nizamur (Bangladesh)
Ḥaḍrat Ṣūfī Fātiḥ ‘Alī Uwaysī (r)	d. 1886 (1304)		Calcutta
Ḥaḍrat Mawlānā Ghulām Salmānī (r)	d. 1912 (1330)		Phuphura (West Bengal)
Ḥaḍrat Sayyid ‘Abd al-Bārī Shāh (r)	1859-1900 (1276-1318)	Balgadhi (Bengal), Calcutta	Bandel (West Bengal)
Ḥaḍrat Ḥāfiẓ Ḥāmid Ḥasan ‘Alawī (r)	1871/72-1959 (1288-1378)		Gonda (India)
Ḥaḍrat Muḥammad Sa‘īd Khān (r)	1907-1976 (1325-1396)		Azamgarh (India)
Ḥaḍrat Azad Rasool (r)	1921-2006 (1339-1426)	Rajastan (India)	Delhi
Ḥaḍrat Ḥāmid Ḥasan	b. 1961 (1380)	Delhi	

Shādhilī	Dates	Place Born or Lived	Place Died
The Prophet Muḥammad ﷺ	570-632 (51 B.H. - 10 A.H.)	Mecca, Medina	Medina
The Caliph Ḥaḍrat ‘Alī ibn Abī Ṭalib	c. 598-661 (c. 24 B.H. - 41 A.H.)	Mecca, Medina	Kūfah
Ḥaḍrat Imām Ḥusayn	626-680 (4-60)	Medina	Karbalā’
Ḥaḍrat Shaykh Muḥammad Jārbadī (r)			
Ḥaḍrat Shaykh Sa‘īd Qīrwānī (r)			
Ḥaḍrat Shaykh Fatiḥ Mas‘ūdī (r)			
Ḥaḍrat Shaykh Abū al-Qāsim Mīrwānī (r)			
Ḥaḍrat Shaykh Abū Isḥāq Ibrāhīm Baṣrī (r)			
Ḥaḍrat Shaykh Quṭbuddīn Mahmūd Qazwīnī (r)			
Ḥaḍrat Shaykh Shamsuddīn (r)			
Ḥaḍrat Shaykh Tājuddīn (r)			
Ḥaḍrat Shaykh Abū al-Ḥasan ‘Alī (r)			
Ḥaḍrat Shaykh Taqīuddīn Ṣūfī (r)			
Ḥaḍrat Shaykh Sharafuddīn Madanī (r)			
Ḥaḍrat Shaykh ‘Abd as-Salām ibn Mashīsh (r)	d. 1228 (625)	Fez	southeast of Tetuan (Morocco)
Ḥaḍrat Shaykh Nūruddīn Abū al-Ḥasan Shādilī (r)	1196-1258 (592-656)	Ghumara (Morocco), Fez, Alexandria (Egypt)	Humaythra (Egypt)
Ḥaḍrat Sayyid ‘Abd al-Bārī Shāh (r)	1859-1900 (1276-1318)	Balgadhi (Bengal), Calcutta	Bandel (West Bengal)
Ḥaḍrat Ḥāfiẓ Ḥāmid Ḥasan ‘Alawī (r)	1871/72-1959 (1288-1378)		Gonda (India)
Ḥaḍrat Muḥammad Sa‘īd Khān (r)	1907-1976 (1325-1396)		Azamgarh (India)
Ḥaḍrat Azad Rasool (r)	1921-2006 (1339-1426)	Rajastan (India)	Delhi
Ḥaḍrat Ḥāmid Ḥasan	b. 1961 (1380)	Delhi	

Chishtī	Dates	Place Born or Lived	Place Died
The Prophet Muḥammad ﷺ	570-632 (51 B.H. - 10 A.H.)	Mecca, Medina	Medina
The Caliph Ḥaḍrat 'Alī ibn Abī Ṭalib ﷺ	c. 598-661 (c. 24 B.H. - 41 A.H.)	Mecca, Medina	Kufah
Ḥaḍrat Ḥasan Baṣrī (r)	642-728 (21-110)	Medina	Basrah
Ḥaḍrat Abū al-Faḍl 'Abd al-Wāḥid ibn Zayd (r)	d. 793 (177)		
Ḥaḍrat Abū al-Fayḍ Fuḍayl ibn 'Iyāḍ (r)	d. 803 (187)		Makkah
Ḥaḍrat Ibrāhīm ibn Adham Balkhī (r)	d. 777/9 (160/2)	Balkh	
Ḥaḍrat Khwājah Sadīduddīn Ḥudhayfah Mar'ashī (r)			
Ḥaḍrat Khwājah Amīnuddīn Abū Hubayrah Baṣrī (r)			Basrah
Ḥaḍrat Khwājah Mamshād 'Ulw Dīnawarī (r)			Dinawar (Persia), Basrah
Ḥaḍrat Khwājah Abū Isḥāq Shāmī Chishtī (r)	d. 940 or 966 (329 or 366)	Syria, Chisht (Afghanistan)	Akka (Syria)
Ḥaḍrat Khwājah Abū Aḥmad ibn Farasnafa (r)	873/4-966 (260-355)	Chisht	Chisht
Ḥaḍrat Khwājah Abū Muḥammad ibn Aḥmad (r)	d. 1020 (411)	Chisht	Chisht
Ḥaḍrat Khwājah Abū Yūsuf Chishtī (r)	985-1066/7 (375-459)	Chisht	Chisht
Ḥaḍrat Muḥammad Mawdūd Chishtī (r)	d. 1133 (527) or 1181/82 (577)	Herat, Balkh, Bukhara	
Ḥaḍrat Ḥajjī Sharīf Zindānī (r)			
Ḥaḍrat Khwājah 'Uthmān Harvanī (r)		Harvan (Nishapur, Persia)	
Ḥaḍrat Khwājah Mu'īnuddīn Chishtī (r)	1142-1236 (537-633)	Seistan (Persia), Ajmer (India), Delhi	Ajmer
Ḥaḍrat Quṭbuddīn Bakhtiyār Kākī (r)	1174-1235 (569-633)	Ush (Transoxania), Delhi	Mihrawli (near Delhi)
Ḥaḍrat Farīduddīn Mas'ūd Ganj-i Shakar (r)	1175-1265 (570-664)	Multan, Hansi, Pakpatan (near Lahore)	Pakpatan
Ḥaḍrat Khwājah Niẓāmuddīn Awliyā' (r)	1243/4-1325 (640/1-726)	Bada'un (east of Delhi)	Delhi
Ḥaḍrat Naṣīruddīn Chirāgh-i Delhī (r)	1276/7-1356 (675-757)	Ayodhya (India), Delhi	Delhi
Ḥaḍrat Kamāluddīn 'Allāma (r)			Gujurat (India)
Ḥaḍrat Sirājuddīn (r)	d. 1411 (814)	Bengal, Delhi	Ahmadabad (India)
Ḥaḍrat 'Ilmuddīn (r)			
Ḥaḍrat Maḥmūd (r)			
Ḥaḍrat Jamāluddīn (r)		Hansi (near Delhi)	
Ḥaḍrat Ḥasan (r)			
Ḥaḍrat Muḥammad (r)			
Ḥaḍrat Muḥammad Yaḥyā Madanī (r)			
Ḥaḍrat Mawlānā Kalīmullāh Jahānābādī (r)	d. 1729 (1142)		Delhi

Ḥaḍrat Mawlānā Niẓāmuddīn (r)			Awrangabad (India)
Ḥaḍrat Mawlānā Fakhruddīn (r)	d. 1784 (1199)		Delhi
Ḥaḍrat Mawlānā Shāh Niyāz Aḥmad (r)	d. 1834 (1250)	Delhi	Bareilly
Ḥaḍrat Mawlānā Shaykh Miskīn (r)			
Ḥaḍrat Mawlānā Nijabet ʻAlī Shāh (r)			
Ḥaḍrat Abū Ḥamid Karīm Bakhsh (r)			
Ḥaḍrat Sayyid ʻAbd al-Bārī Shāh (r)	1859-1900 (1276-1318)	Balgadhi (Bengal), Calcutta	Bandel (West Bengal)
Ḥaḍrat Ḥāfiẓ Ḥāmid Ḥasan ʻAlawī (r)	1871/72-1959 (1288-1378)		Gonda (India)
Ḥaḍrat Muḥammad Saʻīd Khān (r)	1907-1976 (1325-1396)		Azamgarh (India)
Ḥaḍrat Azad Rasool (r)	1921-2006 (1339-1426)	Rajastan (India)	Delhi
Ḥaḍrat Ḥāmid Ḥasan	b. 1961 (1380)	Delhi	

Qādirī	Dates	Place Born or Lived	Place Died
The Prophet Muḥammad ﷺ	570-632 (51 B.H. - 10 A.H.)	Mecca, Medina	Medina
The Caliph Ḥaḍrat ʻAlī ibn Abī Ṭalib ﷺ	c. 598-661 (c. 24 B.H. - 41 A.H.)	Mecca, Medina	Kufah
Ḥaḍrat Imām Ḥusayn ﷺ	626-680 (4-60)	Medina	Karbala'
Ḥaḍrat Imām ʻAlī Zayn al-ʻĀbidīn (r)	d. 712 (93)		
Ḥaḍrat Imām Muḥammad Bāqir (r)	d. 731 (113)		
Ḥaḍrat Imām Jāʻfar aṣ-Ṣādiq (r)	702-765 (83-148)	Medina	Medina
Ḥaḍrat Imām Mūsā al-Kāẓim (r)	d. 799 (183)		
Ḥaḍrat Imām Mūsā Riḍā (r)	d. 818 (202)		
Ḥaḍrat Maʻrūf Karkhī (r)	d. 815/16 (200)	Iran, Baghdad	Baghdad
Ḥaḍrat Sarī Saqaṭī (r)	769-867/68 (152-253)	Baghdad	Baghdad
Ḥaḍrat Junayd Baghdādī (r)	d. 910 (298)	Baghdad	Baghdad
Ḥaḍrat Shaykh Abū Bakr Shiblī (r)	861-946 (247-334)	Baghdad, Samara	Baghdad
Ḥaḍrat Shaykh ʻAbd al-ʻAzīz Tamīmī (r)	d. 634 (425)		
Ḥaḍrat Abū al-Faḍl Abū al-Wāḥid Tamīmī (r)			
Ḥaḍrat Abū al-Faraḥ Tarṭūsī (r)			
Ḥaḍrat Abū al-Ḥasan Farshī (r)	d. 1093 (486)		
Ḥaḍrat Abū Saʻīd al-Mubārak Mukharrimī (r)	d. 1119 (513)		
Ḥaḍrat Shaykh ʻAbd al-Qādir Jīlānī (r)	1077/78-1116	Jilan (Persia) (470-561)	Baghdad
Ḥaḍrat Sayyid ʻAbd al-Bārī Shāh (r)	1859-1900 (1276-1318)	Balgadhi (Bengal), Calcutta	Bandel (West Bengal)
Ḥaḍrat Ḥāfiẓ Ḥāmid Ḥasan ʻAlawī (r)	1871/72-1959 (1288-1378)		Gonda (India)
Ḥaḍrat Muḥammad Saʻīd Khān (r)	1907-1976 (1325-1396)		Azamgarh (India)
Ḥaḍrat Azad Rasool (r)	1921-2006 (1339-1426)	Rajastan (India)	Delhi
Ḥaḍrat Ḥāmid Ḥasan	b. 1961 (1380)	Delhi	

Index

inner aspect (*batin*) xi, 55, 57, 74, 137
inner knowledge (*ma'rifat*) 42, 43, 46, 57, 58, 68, 69, 85, 107, 122, 144
inner world (*anfus*) 19, 153
The Institute of Search for Truth vii, xiii, xvi, 19, 77, 83, 84, 152, 153
intuition 9, 13, 14, 16, 29, 74
Iqbal, Muhammad, 'Allama 94, 143
Islamic law (*shari'a*) xi, 43, 56

J

Jesus 55, 81, 130
jinn 49

K

Kohanda 27, 29, 53, 141, 151

L

Lahore 2, 3, 4, 15, 31

M

madrasa 21, 22, 23
Mangarawan 21, 33, 100
Mathura xviii, xix, 139
Mecca 24, 25, 26, 56, 95, 104
Medina xiii, 24, 26, 56, 87, 114
meditation (*muraqaba*) 14, 17, 28, 34, 40, 48, 50, 58, 59, 64, 65, 66, 67, 78, 79, 80, 83, 95, 96, 98, 99, 100, 102, 105, 114, 115, 142, 155
mental progress 88
miracle(s) (*karamat*) 11, 39, 41, 42, 52, 56, 64, 74, 90, 108, 109, 110, 129, 131
Mitthan Shah 27, 28, 91
Moses xviii, 16, 55, 81, 130, 131
most hidden subtle center (*akhfa*) 49, 54, 55, 66, 130, 135
Muhammad Sai'd Khan iii, xiii, xv, xviii
Mujaddidi/Mujaddidiyya ix, xiii, xv, xvi, 22, 23, 24, 51, 59, 60, 63, 66, 67, 108, 113, 119

N

Naqshband, Hazrat Khwaja Baha'uddin 48, 49, 50, 51, 54, 68, 102
Naqshbandi-Mujaddidi/Naqshbandiyya-Mujaddidiyya ix, xiii, xv, xvi, 23, 24, 60, 67
Naqshbandi/Naqshbandiyya ix, xiii, xv, xvi, 23, 24, 25, 38, 49, 60, 67, 102, 107, 108, 119
nearness to God (*ma'iyyat*) 43, 45, 46, 50, 54, 58, 59, 61, 68, 92, 97, 108, 109, 127, 130
negation and affirmation (*dhikr-i nafi wa-ithbat*) 56, 57, 59, 65, 66, 97

P

person attracted to God (*majdhub*) 90, 91
purification of the heart 18, 43, 51, 95, 122, 135, 136
purification of the self 18, 43, 46, 48, 49, 122

Q

Qadiri/Qadiriyya xii, 63, 66, 67, 119
Qarniyya 112

R

Ramadan x, 21, 24, 104
rationality 8, 9, 10, 13, 14, 18, 108
Rauz ur-Rahman xviii, xix, 16, 109, 139
remembrance of God (*dhikr*) 16, 29, 38, 44, 50, 55, 56, 57, 58, 65, 66, 67, 81, 96, 97, 98, 100, 102, 105, 112, 114, 115, 132, 133
repentance 48, 62, 63, 65, 67, 144
ritual prayer x, 92, 95, 96, 99, 104, 113
Rumi, Jalaluddin xiii, 16, 103, 119

S

Sa'duddin Miyan 36, 40